PIVOTAL
MOMENTS
IN HISTORY

# THE END OF THE SHOGUNS AND THE BIRTH OF MODERN JAPAN

## MARK E. CUNNINGHAM & LAWRENCE J. ZWIER

TWENTY-FIRST CENTURY BOOKS
MINNEAPOLIS

*To Our Children: Daniel Cunningham and Maryn and Robbie Zwier*

Consultant: John Mock, Ph.D., Doctoral Program in International Public Policy, College of International Studies, University of Tsukuba, Japan

Primary source material in this text is printed over an antique-paper texture.

*Front cover: This Japanese print (c.1818–1820) shows the samurai warriors Ichijo Jiro Tadanori and Notonokami Noritsune fighting.*

Twenty-First Century Books
A division of Lerner Publishing Group, Inc.
241 First Avenue North
Minneapolis, MN 55401 U.S.A.

Website address: www.lernerbooks.com

Library of Congress Cataloging-in-Publication Data

Cunningham, Mark E.
    The end of the shoguns and the birth of modern Japan / by Mark E. Cunningham and Lawrence J. Zwier.
        p.   cm. — (Pivotal moments in history)
    Includes bibliographical references and index.
    ISBN 978–0–8225–8747–7 (lib. bdg. : alk. paper)
    1. Japan—History—1787–1868—Juvenile literature. 2. Japan—History—Restoration, 1853–1870—Juvenile literature. I. Zwier, Lawrence J. II. Title.
DS881.3.C86 2009
952'.025—dc22                                                            2008026871

Manufactured in the United States of America
1 2 3 4 5 6 – BP – 14 13 12 11 10 09

# CONTENTS

# CHAPTER ONE
# Beginnings

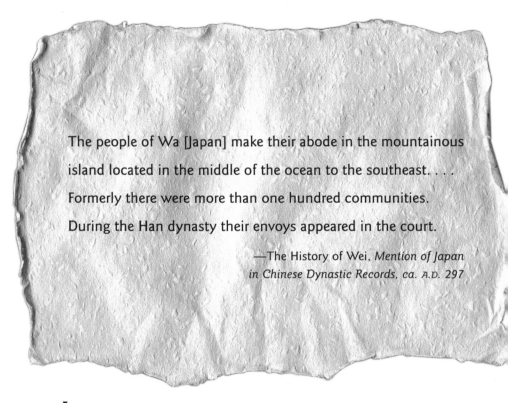

The people of Wa [Japan] make their abode in the mountainous island located in the middle of the ocean to the southeast. . . . Formerly there were more than one hundred communities. During the Han dynasty their envoys appeared in the court.

—The History of Wei, *Mention of Japan in Chinese Dynastic Records, ca. A.D. 297*

It is November 1868, and Japan is welcoming the emperor to Edo, soon to become the official capital of Japan. The teenage emperor's procession crosses a bridge over the moat into the great palace. The journey from Kyoto had been long. Everywhere, awestruck crowds had been silent as the closed compartment carrying their ruler passed. Few could have imagined they would live to see an emperor traveling among them.

The Edo palace is massive. The shoguns, its former

occupants, had ruled the land for more than 250 years. They are gone, driven from power by men who gladly shed their blood to restore the emperor as the heart and soul of the nation. The name the teenaged emperor chose for his reign was Meiji, or "enlightened rule." The years of his life and his reign will see dramatic events that will put his people on a path from isolation to world power. This pivotal moment in history is known as the Meiji Restoration.

The story of Japan's emperors begins in legend, with the mythical descent of the first emperor, Jimmu, from the sun goddess Amaterasu, traditionally dated to the sixth century B.C. Dates in traditional chronicles are considered unreliable

This print, made in Japan about 1868, shows the procession of Emperor Meiji into the Edo palace. The emperor rides in the closed sedan chair near the center of the bridge.

until the reign of the twenty-ninth emperor, Kimmei, from 539 to 571. An unbroken lineage to the modern-day imperial family is said to date from his reign.

Japan's four main islands—Kyushu, Shikoku, Honshu, and Hokkaido—and its many smaller islands lie off the northeastern coast of Asia. Japan's geographical isolation and its topography have strongly influenced its history. Fertile land for farming can be found in a few large plains and in Japan's countless valleys, but much of the country is covered by mountain forests and divided by mountain ridges.

A Chinese chronicle of A.D. 297 describes the land of Wa. From A.D. 250 to 538, the beginnings of a Japanese state developed around Nara (north of modern-day Osaka). Local leaders had gained control of farming villages, which then developed into chiefdoms, or small kingdoms. Early rulers gradually brought the chiefdoms in central and western Honshu and parts of Kyushu under their control.

From 538 to 710, Buddhism, Confucianism, and Taoism came to Japan from China. The Japanese adopted Chinese written characters, and Japanese rulers created a centralized state under an emperor, using the Chinese model.

## THE EMPERORS

By the Nara Period (710 to 784), the emperors controlled most of what was then considered Japan. The people of northern Honshu and Hokkaido were thought of as non-Japanese barbarians.

In addition to running the state, an emperor also had important spiritual functions. Considered divine because of the imperial line's descent from the sun goddess, the emperor communicated with *kami*, the nature gods of the Shinto religion, to ensure the welfare of the people. A refined

# RELIGIONS IN JAPAN

The early Japanese worshipped the spirits of natural features and forces, such as mountains, trees, animals, or rivers. These folk beliefs developed into Shinto—"the way of the gods."

Buddhism came to Japan from India. It teaches people how to overcome earthly suffering through enlightenment. Buddhism in Japan developed into many sects, or groups with distinctive beliefs and practices. At times, Buddhist sects and monasteries became powerful political and military forces.

Chinese Taoism emphasizes harmony with the powers and mysteries of the universe. It was well received in Japan, often blending with the ancient folk beliefs of Shinto.

Confucianism also came to Japan from China. Confucianism is more of a philosophy and a system of ethical teachings than a religion. It stresses moral conduct, obedience within the home, and respect for those in authority as the basis of a good society.

The many religious and philosophical beliefs in Japan generally coexisted and often influenced one another. Japanese people see no contradiction in having their marriages blessed at Shinto shrines and having Buddhist funerals.

culture flourished in the new imperial capital of Kyoto, encouraging uniquely Japanese arts and literature.

By the eleventh century, imperial authority began to decline. The emperor became less an actual ruler than a symbol that others were eager to control. Great noble families could protect and expand their power by marriage with the imperial family or by positioning family members as regents who ruled in the name of a child heir to the throne.

## THE SAMURAI

Japan's emperors also saw their authority weakened by the rise of a warrior class. The word *samurai* originally meant "those who serve" the emperor, but it came to refer increasingly to warriors who served and fought for local lords. These lords were themselves warriors and clan leaders. They rewarded their followers with lands and incomes. The emperors could not control the growing power of lords backed by their samurai armies and found it increasingly difficult to rule them.

The samurai evolved a code of conduct called Bushido, the way of the warrior. Along with a stoic acceptance of suffering and death, a fundamental samurai value was loyalty in serving their masters with their fighting skills. Samurai lived for war and deserved their reputation as some of the deadliest warriors in history. Their preferred fighting technique of archery on horseback shifted over time to lethal sword fighting. With samurai warriors helping lords fight among themselves to assert local independence and dominate neighbors, Japan would know little peace.

This image from the late 1700s shows two samurai. Each has armor and two swords. The samurai on the right has a quiver of arrows, and the samurai on the left has set his helmet and sword on the ground.

## THE GREAT GENERAL

As imperial power declined, great families and clans struggled for power. Minamoto Yoritomo eventually established his Minamoto clan as the supreme military power in Japan. In 1185 he had the emperor appoint him *seiidaishogun*. This was originally the title of a great general who led the emperor's armies in subduing the so-called barbarians in northeastern Honshu. Minamoto Yoritomo was the first of Japan's ruling shoguns.

At the time that Yoritomo established his shogunal government in Kamakura, a feudal system was taking root. In this system, local lords commanded obedience and income from the subjects in their domains, the lands they controlled. The local lords were in turn vassals, or subjects, of the shogun. They owed him obedience and military support when he required it.

Beginning with Yoritomo's appointment, the shogun was able to pass his title and powers to a designated heir. To keep this inheritance within the Minamoto family, the shoguns often adopted—usually from other branches of the family—capable successors for inherited titles. The emperors continued to formally approve the shoguns' titles. But political and military power in Japan lay with the shoguns and those who could control their governments.

The first shogunate faced many problems. Rebellious lords were never brought completely under control. Conflict broke out when the imperial court briefly reasserted itself. Choosing a new shogun often involved family and court intrigues and rivalries. Outsiders used the shogunate to further their own power and influence. At times the shoguns seemed to be mere figureheads.

Despite its weaknesses, the Minamoto family shogunate at Kamakura lasted from 1192 to 1333 and provided Japan with some stability. It could mobilize forces to meet challenges such as the invasions in 1274 and 1281 by the Mongols of central Asia, who had taken control of China. These invasions failed after encountering spirited Japanese resistance and typhoons (tropical storms) that scattered the invasion fleets.

The shoguns of the Ashikaga clan succeeded the Minamoto shogunate. The Ashikaga found it more difficult

# JAPANESE NAMES

Japanese names are usually given with names of families first—including clans and dynasties such as the Minamoto—followed by the personal name. In many histories, a person's complete name is usually given in the first mention. After that, the personal name is often used alone. Readers will first encounter the name Toyotomi Hideyoshi, then after that see the person referred to as simply Hideyoshi to distinguish that person from others with the same family name. However, in modern times, people who do not belong to one of the Japanese dynasties are usually referred to by their family name after their full names are given.

to control increasingly powerful local rulers—the daimyo, or great names—and their samurai. Rival clans fought to influence and control the shogunate and the imperial court. As the breakdown of shogunal authority deepened, Japan experienced more than a century of civil war and disorder—the Sengoku, or "Warring States" period.

## THE COMING OF THE EUROPEANS

In 1543 two Portuguese traders came ashore at Tanegashima Island (near Kyushu) after their ship was blown off course. They were soon followed by more traders and by Catholic missionaries (religious teachers) led by the Spanish Jesuit priest Francis Xavier in 1549.

Japan traded openly with foreigners. Japanese merchants and sailors traveled throughout eastern Asia. Japanese traders and mercenary soldiers (soldiers hired to fight) could be found as far away as the Philippines and Siam (Thailand). Trade through southwestern Japan and through the Ryukyu Islands brought luxuries from China, Korea, and even Southeast Asia.

Japanese traders on the China coast became a problem. The Japanese smuggled goods and, as fearsome pirates called *wako*, they threatened coastal shipping when trade was slow. To keep the pirates and their raids away, China's emperors banned overseas commerce and seafaring. Stern laws were made against trade with Japan. The Chinese, however, tolerated the Portuguese as middlemen. Operating from Macao on the China coast, the Portuguese carried mainly Chinese cargoes to Japan and Japanese products to China.

The crumbling of the shogunate's authority during the Warring States period meant that locally powerful lords could deal freely with the European *nanban*, or "southern barbarians," so called because they had come to Japan from the south. Crude as the Europeans seemed, the Japanese saw that much was to be gained through contact with them.

As the Christian missionaries spread through Japan, some Japanese found promise in this new religion. The missionaries made many converts, particularly in southwestern Japan. Some daimyo converted too—or at least seemed sympathetic. There were advantages in letting missionaries preach in their domains and cultivating the goodwill of the foreigners. The Europeans brought not only religion but also the gun.

The first Portuguese to land in Japan sparked the interest of a local lord by demonstrating the European harquebus. This large-bore musket had a fuse that burned down to ignite the gunpowder. It could dominate the battlefield. Skilled

Japanese artisans copied the weapons and quickly learned how to make guns and gunpowder. The European guns helped shape the course of Japanese history.

## THE UNIFIERS

As Europeans and European influences were arriving, the weakened Ashikaga shogunate was coming to an end. Three remarkable men rose to power in this era and unified Japan.

One ambitious noble, Oda Nobunaga, expanded his power base by crushing his rivals. A major reason for his success was the early and skillful use of firearms. The volleys of massed

*This painting, made on a silk folding screen in the mid-1500s, shows the arrival of the Portuguese in Japan.*

soldiers equipped with the harquebus could smash the armies of his enemies. Oda soon controlled central Japan. In 1569 he took over Kyoto, assuming what little governing power the emperor had left. The weak Ashikaga shogun unsuccessfully rebelled. He was exiled, the last of a troubled line.

In 1582 Oda Nobunaga died after being betrayed by an ally. Japan had lost a forceful ruler and a man of vision. Oda had placed Japan on a path out of chaos and toward a new kind of strong ruler who could unite Japan.

Oda's powers were assumed by one of his generals, Toyotomi Hideyoshi. Building on Oda's successes, Hideyoshi extended his military control of Japan. He was equally skilled in defeating his opponents and getting them to accept his rule as allies. After the exiled Ashikaga shogun died, Hideyoshi assumed political and military control over Japan. His common birth prevented him from receiving the title of shogun, so he ruled with the lesser title of *kampaku*.

Hideyoshi formalized the status of samurai by decreeing that they had to be full-time warriors (not part-time farmers) and always prepared for military service to their lords. He needed these ready forces in his drive to unify Japan. As a security measure, he limited the bearing of arms to the warrior class and conducted "sword hunts" to disarm all nonsamurai.

He also ordered surveys of productive lands and the wealth they produced, measured in *koku,* or the amount of rice an adult could eat in a year. The surveys helped determine the wealth of vassal lords and how many samurai they could support. Wealthier vassals owed more in military service and other obligations. This valuable knowledge aided Hideyoshi in his quest for peace through unification of Japan.

Japan

RUSSIA

CHINA

NORTH
KOREA

Sea of
Japan

JAPAN

HOKKAIDO

Hakodate

Akita

AIZU

Niigata

ECHIZEN

HIKONE

HONSHU

Mito
Edo
(Tokyo)

Yokohama
Kamakura

Edo
(Tokyo)
Bay

SOUTH
KOREA

Shimonoseki

CHOSHU

AKI

Hyogo
(Kobe)

Kyoto

OWARI

Shimoda

Tsushima
Strait

Osaka

Toba

TSUSHIMA

Shimonoseki Strait

Ise

SHIKOKU

HIZEN

KYUSHU

TOSA

Nagasaki

UWA

Kagoshima

SATSUMA

TANEGASHIMA

Province

International border

Tokaido (highway)

Capital city

City

RYUKYU ISLANDS

PACIFIC
OCEAN

OKINAWA

Naha

Miles

0    50    100    150

0    100    200

Kilometers

# CHAPTER TWO

# THE TOKUGAWA SECURITY STATE

Japanese ships are forbidden to leave Japan. . . . No Japanese is permitted to go abroad. If there is anyone who does so secretly, he must be executed.

Portuguese . . . ships must be destroyed and anyone aboard those ships must be beheaded.

—*Tokugawa Iemitsu, Edicts of 1635 and 1639*

In 1598 the dying Hideyoshi appointed Tokugawa Ieyasu as one of the regents for his son. Ieyasu was an important daimyo who had served Oda in his rise to power. After crushing his rivals at the Battle of Sekigahara in 1600, Ieyasu solidified his power by rewarding supporters and by either punishing enemies or negotiating their obedience. Tokugawa Ieyasu was made shogun by the emperor in 1603.

Up until his death in 1616, Ieyasu worked to make sure the

shogunate would remain in his family. Ruthless and politically shrewd, the Tokugawas became unrivaled masters of Japan, with the military power and the title needed to back up their rule. The Tokugawa shogunate would rule for more than two and a half centuries and bring Japan one of its longest periods of peace and stability.

A portrait of Tokugawa Ieyasu, painted in Japan in the 1600s

Having won their wars, the Tokugawas now had to govern Japan and maintain their power. Ieyasu had confirmed many changes undertaken by Oda Nobunaga and Toyotomi Hideyoshi to end Japan's state of chronic warfare. Japan would keep its feudal system, but with the daimyo under their control so that they could never again tear the country apart. Vassal lords would employ their own samurai and would tax and govern their domains locally. They would provide military support when summoned by the shogun. With loyal vassals and their samurai directly under their control, the Tokugawas brought a new level of national unity to Japan. Disobedient daimyo found themselves attacked, stripped of their domains, or relocated. Some were ordered to take their own lives through seppuku, or ritual suicide—a dignity permitted members of the warrior class.

# SUICIDE BY DECREE

A daimyo or samurai guilty of serious political offenses could preserve his honor and his family's standing by taking his own life. Isaac Titsingh, a Dutch official at Deshima in the late 1700s, describes seppuku ordered by the shogunate as punishment:

As soon as the order of the court has been communicated . . . the culprit invites his intimate friends for the appointed day, and regales them with sake [rice wine]. After they have drunk together . . . he takes leave of them, and the order of the court is read once more . . . in the presence of their secretary and the inspector. The person . . . then addresses a speech or compliment to the company, after which he inclines his head towards the mat, draws his saber and cuts himself across the belly, penetrating to his bowels. One of his confidential servants . . . then strikes off his head. Such as wish to display superior courage, after the cross cut inflict a second longitudinally, and then a third in the throat. No disgrace is attached to such a death, and the son succeeds to his father's place.

The shogunate defined and controlled all levels of society. Ieyasu—following Hideyoshi's division of Japanese society—confirmed for centuries a system of four distinct classes. Merchants were the lowest rank, next came artisans, and then farmers. At the top of the class system was the hereditary warrior class—the samurai and their lords. Along with these divisions came laws formalizing what each class could and could not do, as well as regulating people's occupations. The shogunate made rules about clothing, hairstyles, and even the food the different classes could eat. Samurai, for example, traditionally carried two swords, wore armor, and tied their hair back in a large topknot. Each class was told in great detail which fabrics they could wear and how their marriages were to be arranged. Families were required to register at Buddhist temples to make it easier to keep track of the population.

## THE CHRISTIAN THREAT

The ships of other European powers followed the Portuguese into trade with Asia. As the shoguns watched the trade empires of the Christian Europeans expanding through a mix of commerce, religion, and military power, they became suspicious. They questioned the loyalty of Japanese converts to Christianity and the intentions of Portuguese and Spanish missionaries. Particularly in southwestern Japan, many had converted to the foreign religion, even a few daimyo. Some of the daimyo were no doubt sincere about their interest in Christianity, while others had seen it as a way to cement foreign trade connections.

Christianity was seen as a threat to the Tokugawas. They were concerned that Japanese Christians might owe their loyalty to their foreign god and the Europeans who had brought the new religion. Missionaries were expelled or imprisoned, tortured, and executed along with their Japanese converts.

A peasant rebellion on Kyushu's Shimabara Peninsula from 1637 to 1638 was brutally crushed after fierce resistance. The uprising involved many Christians, and the shogunate suspected the involvement of foreign countries. The Tokugawas decided that Christianity must be rooted out.

Eliminating the threat of the Europeans and their religion meant sharply limiting Japan's outside contacts. The country turned its back on almost a century of dealing with European merchants and missionaries. The shogun also limited and closely controlled trade with China and Korea. The Tokugawas made the question of who was allowed to enter, leave, or spread their ideas in Japan a matter of national security. Laws ended most trade carried in foreign ships, overseas voyages by Japanese ships, and foreign travel by Japanese.

Punishments were fierce. Japanese attempting to leave Japan or return from overseas would be executed. To discourage overseas commerce, trade within Japan could only be carried in small coastal vessels. The daimyo were restricted in the kind of ships they could maintain for their own defense. The final edict to close Japan came in 1639, after Japan accused the Portuguese of secretly bringing in and helping missionary priests and friars. The edict clearly stated the punishments for European intrusions: Ships would be burned. Crews and passengers would be beheaded. In an unmistakable warning, most members of a delegation to Japan from Portuguese Macao were put to death the following year.

By the mid-1600s, the shogunate had completed the near-isolation of Japan from foreign countries. Limited Chinese trade was allowed through Nagasaki. Some trade with Korea was permitted. Among Europeans, only Dutch traders were allowed to bring a few ships a year to their outpost on the tiny artificial island of Deshima at Nagasaki. This would be Japan's main contact with the West for more than two centuries. The Dutch—along with British traders—had arrived after the Spanish and Portuguese. The Dutch seemed less threatening than the Catholic Portuguese. The Protestant Dutch did not engage in missionary activities and were mainly interested in profits. They even had been useful to the shogun, helping him bombard besieged rebels on the Shimabara Peninsula in 1637 to 1638.

The shogunate froze or even reversed recent advances in military and shipping technology. The firearms that had helped bring the Tokugawas to power fell out of favor. The samurai's two swords would continue as the symbol of the Japanese warrior for another two centuries. Japanese shipbuilders, whose skills could produce a perfect copy of a Spanish galleon capable of crossing the Pacific, were allowed to build only small coastal vessels.

Thus ended the days of the nanban trade—commerce with and through the southern barbarians. The religion and the ships from the West were no longer welcome. Japan's part in a growing, seaborne world economy was over, choked down to an easily controlled trickle. This was the closing of Japan and the beginning of the country's isolation. It was intended to protect the country from turmoil and outsiders.

While internal political change would be rigidly controlled, Japanese society was anything but stagnant. The great peace of the Tokugawas allowed important social, cultural, and economic developments. Japan entered a period of relative prosperity and growth, with no major conflicts for 250 years.

## ATTENDANCE, CASTLES, AND LAND

Under Tokugawa Ieyasu's son Hidetada, the Tokugawas established Japan's political capital in Edo. Edo grew to be the world's largest city, with over one million inhabitants.

Edo was central to Tokugawa control of Japan. The shoguns forced most daimyo to travel to Edo and attend the shogunal court every other year. This system of *sankin kotai*, or alternate attendance, helped the shogun keep an eye on the lords in Edo. It also forced daimyo to spend heavily to keep their households and retainers (attendants) in suitable style in Edo and on grand processions from their domains to Edo and back. Little money was left for military preparations

*A daimyo on his way to the emperor's court parades through the streets of Kyoto with his samurai and servants. A Japanese artist painted this picture about 1700.*

"Someone shouted in an exaggeratedly loud voice 'oranda kapitan' to prompt him to step forward and pay his respects. Thereupon he crawled forward on his hands and knees between the place where the presents had been lined up and the high seat of his majesty. . . . Crouching on his knees, he bent his head to the floor and then, like a lobster, crawled back in this very same position, without one word being exchanged. This short, miserable procedure is all that there is to this famous audience. Nothing else happens at the annual audience of the important territorial lords."

—Engelbert Koempher, describing a Dutch official's audience with the shogun in the 1690s

that might threaten the shogunate. Good behavior was guaranteed by requiring absent daimyo to leave their families in Edo as hostages to the shogun. For the upper classes, Edo also provided shared experiences and a sense of national identity. Daimyo and their retainers enjoyed its lively cultural life, attended the grand ceremonies, and served in positions of responsibility in the government.

The Tokugawas further weakened the daimyo by allowing them to have only one major castle in their domains. Castles had been important strongholds in the warfare of earlier periods and were symbols of daimyo power. The castle towns became administrative and cultural centers. In the early Tokugawa period, the daimyo were forced to contribute to major projects such as the building of Chiyoda Castle in Edo.

Tokugawa rule rested on reliable domains ruled by related family branches or by families that were loyal Tokugawa vassals. The founder of Tokugawa power, Ieyasu, had stripped troublesome daimyo of their domains or reduced their holdings. He even removed some and replaced them with loyal vassals and allies. The Tokugawa shoguns had enormous landholdings as their financial base. They also obtained revenues by controlling trade in copper, silver, and gold.

All Japanese society was monitored by a suspicious shogunate. To keep order, the Tokugawa state relied on local samurai forces of the domains, an effective secret police network, and ferocious punishments. In the upper reaches of society, officials kept a watchful eye out for signs of dissatisfaction and plots among daimyo and within the imperial court.

The shogunate discouraged unnecessary travel and required the travelers to show documents at checkpoints as they moved from area to area. The Tokugawas' social vision held that farming, not commerce, was the basis of society. Farmers were so important that they belonged to the second-highest rank of social classes. Because of their importance, farmers were not allowed to leave the land they farmed.

Samurai were required to wear their two swords and to train for war, but under the Tokugawa peace, they had few opportunities to fight. Not all was peaceful, however. There was little to protect citizens from the blades of easily insulted warriors swaggering through city streets or escorting their lords on the highways. Authorities dealt harshly with brawls between samurai swordsmen or unrest of any sort.

The Tokugawas surveyed and regulated nearly every

aspect of economic and social life. For tax purposes and to help control the countryside, villages were organized into units and smaller neighborhood associations. Members had to watch one another and sometimes shared punishments for their neighbors' crimes. Requiring families to register their members at Buddhist temples provided a means of control as well as useful information.

Ieyasu continued the practice of measuring the land wealth and incomes of the daimyo and their retainers in koku of rice. This set the value of lands held by vassals and the amount of military support the shogun could expect from them. The rule setting incomes in rice contributed to the rise of an urban merchant class. These merchants advanced loans to vassals for salaries they would earn in rice when the crop came in. Samurai often owed money to merchant-class moneylenders. Unlike their lords, samuari could not always use their positions to avoid repaying their debts.

## SOCIETY IN TOKUGAWA JAPAN

The first half of the Tokugawa period saw economic expansion, a rise in population, and the growth of cities. Classes were rigidly defined, but some social movement took place within them. Farmers were the backbone of the nation. Artisans made tools and produced luxuries for the samurai and daimyo as well as the growing merchant class in the cities. The samurai lived as well as they could on the declining value of their incomes.

Not all samurai were idle. Some found work guarding barriers on highways. Samurai of the middle and higher ranks were often employed as administrators in the castle towns. Some poor samurai ignored the laws and engaged in business or farming or took up crafts that were not specifically banned.

Despite the shogunate's limits on travel, great highways such as the Tokaido were alive with commercial transport by packhorse. (Wheeled vehicles were banned from the major roads, so coastal shipping transported bulk goods such as rice and timber.) Huge processions accompanied daimyo going to and from required attendance at Edo. Nobles and retainers exchanged their rice-based incomes for gold or silver money to pay for traveling to Edo and living there. Pilgrims thronged the roads to famous Shinto sites such as the one at Ise. Rest stops on Japan's great highways became famous for offering pleasures of all kinds to travelers.

## EDO PERIOD CULTURE

As transportation networks expanded, cultural life, as well as markets, extended beyond the main cities to the merchants and samurai of the castle towns and even smaller communities. Kabuki theater was popular. Originally featuring only dance, kabuki performances had become stylized dramatic plays. Wood-block prints—blocks of wood with scenes carved into them that were printed on paper in vibrant color—reached a peak during this time. Literature flourished. Poets such as Basho celebrated Japan's landscapes and seasons. New forms of novels emerged and reached a broader audience as literacy spread. Even merchants and prosperous farmers could read and write. By the end of the Tokugawa period, Japan had one of the highest literacy rates in the world.

In this wood-block print from the late 1700s, kabuki actors perform in a theater before an eager audience.

# HAIKU BY BASHO

Matsuo Basho is perhaps the best-known composer of haiku, a short poem with a fixed number of syllables. From a poor samurai background, Basho established himself in Edo, living simply and experimenting with verse. In the years before his death in 1697, he traveled Japan's roads and wrote movingly of the scenes he encountered in *The Narrow Road to the Deep North*:

27

Sitting at full ease
On the doors of their huts
The fishermen enjoy
A cool evening.

Shinto, with its ever-present nature gods worshipped in local Shinto shrines, enjoyed a revival from the mid-1700s on. A growing religious and nationalistic movement rejected "foreign" Buddhist beliefs in favor of the native religion. Hirata Atsutane of the Akita domain and other intellectuals wanted Japan to return to fundamentals, to the way of the gods and reverence for the emperor. They felt Buddhist practices should be separated from Shinto. The Confucian beliefs of the ruling elites should stress that Japanese owed their first loyalty and obedience to the emperor.

In the 1700s, the shogunate relaxed its ban on foreign books. This inspired a handful of Japanese to learn Dutch to better understand Western science. These scholars translated "Dutch learning" into Japanese. Their study of Western works in such areas as anatomy provided a window on scientific and technical developments in the West.

## JAPAN ON THE EVE OF CHANGE

An observer in the early 1800s looking back might feel that the 250 years of Tokugawa rule had been a success. The shogunate's rule had changed little for over two centuries. Samurai loyally served their daimyo. The daimyo acknowledged that the authority of the shogun held Japan together and had to be obeyed absolutely. The emperor was a misty, distant figure in Kyoto, but the real power structure of the shogunate protected a stable, flourishing Japan.

The Tokugawa government endured. But weaknesses in the social structure and new dangers from the outside were becoming apparent by the start of the nineteenth century. Suffering deepened in rural areas when bad harvests caused famines. Hard economic times caused protests in cities and rural areas against heavy taxation by domain governments. The feudal system of government dividing authority between the shogunate and the domains was showing signs of strain. At the same time, some intellectuals were beginning to question the Tokugawas' right to rule.

The outer domains, particularly those in the southwest, which had been on the losing side against Ieyasu, still resented the Tokugawas. Kept weak to prevent them from challenging the shogun, most of these domains were poorly prepared to defend the country. The weakness of the entire system of Tokugawa rule was about to be exposed by an old menace sailing in once again from over the horizon. The southern barbarians were coming back.

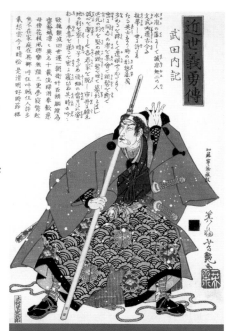

This woodcut shows a daimyo in formal clothes. He carries two swords and a spear. Japanese artist Utagawa Toyokuni created this woodcut in the early 1800s.

# CHAPTER THREE
# OPENING JAPAN

Last summer the American barbarians arrived in the Bay of
Uruga with four warships, bearing their president's message.
Their deportment and manner of expression were exceedingly
arrogant, and the resulting insult to our national dignity was
not small. Those who heard could only gnash their teeth.

—*Sakuma Shozan, Japanese scholar, 1854*

In 1808 the British frigate HMS *Phaeton* sailed into the
harbor at Nagasaki and approached the Dutch outpost of
Deshima. At the time, Great Britain and France were at
war. Since France controlled the Netherlands, the British
navy felt free to attack Dutch shipping. But no Dutch
vessels were in port, so there was nothing for the British
to attack and plunder. Instead, they took Dutch hostages,
demanded supplies at gunpoint, and left before Japanese

defense forces could assemble. The ease of this intrusion shocked the shogunate. The government quickly reaffirmed the policy of exclusion, tried to improve coastal defenses, and issued new edicts requiring immediate death for any foreigners landing. The daimyo responsible for Nagasaki's defense committed suicide.

In the early nineteenth century, the shogunate received increasing reports of parties from Western ships landing in search of water or firewood. Naha, on the island of Okinawa just south of the main islands of Japan, was visited by whaling ships from the United States and Europe. Villages on Hokkaido were too.

The Tokugawa leadership was aware of developments outside of Japan. A few scholars in Japan learned of technological advances in the West by way of translated Dutch learning from the Dutch outpost at Nagasaki. The shoguns knew of the European powers' push for trade and control of trade areas in eastern Asia, particularly in China.

The greatest threat to Japan was Great Britain. Britain was the world's leading trading and naval power. British merchant ships took Britain's manufactured goods around the world, and the commerce and wealth of the world's nations flowed back to Britain. Elsewhere in Asia, the British had taken over European outposts in other Asian countries and were prying China open to trade through war, threats, and treaties.

The Russian Empire was another menace to Japan. It had expanded across Asia and had reached the northern shores of the Pacific. Russian fur trappers and explorers roamed the islands to the north of Japan, and Russian ships were increasingly present in Japanese waters.

By the mid-1800s, the United States, too, was becoming a Pacific power. The United States had expanded to the Pacific by annexing (taking over) the Oregon Territory and then acquiring California following the Mexican-American War (1846–1848). The U.S. purchase of Russian Alaska in 1867 and its interest in the Polynesian kingdom of Hawaii helped to solidify the U.S. position in the Pacific.

## THE LESSON OF CHINA

Neighboring China—long the greatest power in eastern Asia and an empire that had believed itself the center of the world—was on its knees at the hands of the despised Westerners. Rather than colonizing and ruling China outright, countries such as Great Britain used limited military actions and threats to gain economic and diplomatic advantages. Sometimes the British seized strategic territory. Using unequal treaties, which heavily favored the foreign powers, Great Britain and other western powers could demand trade on their terms.

The British had humiliated the Chinese in the First Opium War (1839–1842). China had tried to stop imports of opium (an addictive drug) from British India after millions of Chinese had become addicted to it. The British would not tolerate this interference with trade, which threatened British profits. British fleets, superior firepower, and efficient military organization defeated the crumbling Chinese dynasty. Hong Kong Island was taken from China and made a British trading outpost. The Chinese were forced to open ports to the British and make concessions that allowed British trade and other privileges in China. The Tokugawas knew Japan could be next.

The dimensions of this sort of disaster heading for Japan were becoming clearer. Seaborne commerce and naval power were growing thanks to the new steam-driven, coal-fired ships that could power through any weather, greatly reducing the time needed for voyages. Western warships could steam in and bombard Asian shores at will, unafraid of being trapped by unfavorable winds.

Clearly, the Tokugawa policy of national seclusion would be hard to maintain. The shogunate was unsure how to respond to the Europeans' threatening presence near their shores and their aggressive demands for trade concessions and trading outposts. First, it threatened terrible punishments for any foreigners setting foot in Japan. Then it made halfhearted concessions for provisioning foreign ships.

## AMERICANS IN JAPAN

Since the late 1700s, the United States had been a growing presence in Asia. U.S. ships had been sailing past Japan to trade with China. U.S. ships had even taken cargoes to Deshima under the Dutch flag in the late 1700s and early 1800s. U.S. ships were also active in the profitable whale and fur seal hunts in the Pacific Ocean and the Sea of Okhotsk (north of Hokkaido). As U.S. shipping and whaling increased, the humane treatment of shipwrecked American sailors was a growing concern for the U.S. government.

Vessels from the United States had picked up Japanese sailors who had been stranded or whose boats had blown off course or sunk. In 1837 a U.S. merchant ship based in China, the *Morrison*, had tried to return shipwrecked Japanese sailors and use the opportunity to establish trade and missionary contacts. The ship was driven off by cannon fire near Edo and again at Kagoshima. In 1845 Japan had allowed a U.S. whaling ship to land shipwrecked Japanese sailors near Edo. Then it was sternly ordered to leave and never return.

In 1846 an attempt by U.S. commander James Biddle to open trade relations failed. Reportedly, Japanese authorities insulted him and then towed his two warships out of Tokyo Bay. In 1848 the threat of force helped U.S. captain James Glynn rescue shipwrecked U.S. seamen held at Nagasaki. On his return to the United States, Glynn recommended that the United States send a strong naval force to open relations. Many factors made this seem like a good idea. These included the desire to end the imprisonment of U.S. sailors shipwrecked in Japan and the growing need to provision and refuel U.S. shipping in the Pacific. The United States had increasing interest in the Pacific region. Americans had a growing confidence that the United States was destined to expand west.

## THE PERRY EXPEDITION

In 1852 U.S. president Millard Fillmore directed Commodore Matthew Calbraith Perry and the U.S. Navy to prepare an armed expedition to Japan. Their objectives were to safeguard the welfare of U.S. sailors and vessels and open peaceful relations. The challenging mission would combine armed force and diplomacy.

The Japan Expedition made careful preparations. But American knowledge of Japan was limited and outdated. Much of it was drawn from the incomplete and only somewhat reliable accounts of Europeans working for the Dutch at Deshima—Isaac Titsingh, Peter Carl Thunberg, and even Engelbert Kaempfer (whose observations were 150 years old). Aside from hazy notions of a popelike religious emperor in Kyoto and a governing emperor in Edo handling practical affairs, the United Sates knew little about the political situation in Japan or how decisions were made.

The expedition had no competent translators. A few people could read Chinese-based Japanese writing. But not one American on the expedition spoke Japanese fluently. Japanese castaways, who had been rescued and ended up as sailors on U.S. vessels, did valuable service as informal translators. But they knew nothing about business contracts or treaty terms. Dutch and Chinese, as well as Japanese and English, were the official languages in treaty negotiations.

The expedition did not include a single professional diplomat. Perry, who saw the world through the eyes of a naval officer, had made sure he was running the show, backed by four modern and dangerous-looking U.S. Navy warships. Aware of Japanese attacks on foreign vessels near Japan's shores and of the importance of Perry's mission, the Americans would arrive ready for anything.

## HARD CHOICES

Perry's four warships arrived at Uraga, near the entrance to Edo Bay (Tokyo Bay) in 1853. Nervous local officials told the Americans to go away and try again at Nagasaki. But Perry landed with a show of force and impressive ceremony. Then he presented his letter of introduction to official representatives

Commodore Perry's troops make the first landing at Edo Bay in 1853. In this 1855 print from the United States, two samurai stand in front of a ship flying the emperor's black-and-white flag. Behind them, Perry leads a line of blue-coated officers greeting Japanese officials.

of the shogunate, along with a letter from President Fillmore. Fillmore requested that shipwrecked U.S. sailors be well treated and allowed to return home and that U.S. ships be allowed to take on provisions. Most importantly, Fillmore declared that the United States and Japan should open friendly relations.

Perry, with full powers to negotiate a treaty, made it clear to the Japanese that he expected an official—and favorable—response. Before sailing for the China coast, he told the Japanese officials that he would return for that response the following spring with a larger force.

The visit caused panic in Edo. Perry's departure left Japan's leadership facing some of the most difficult decisions in Japanese history. There was no choice but to respond to Perry's demands. Shogun Ieyoshi was dying, and major shogunate decisions of this sort were usually handled by a group of senior councillors. The uncomfortable task of responding to the Americans fell to the chief councillor, Abe Masahiro.

By even allowing Perry to land and present his letters, the shogunate had broken its seclusion policy of more than two centuries. Abe took the unusual step of seeking the views of the daimyo on the difficult question of what to do

"On the arrival of the Commodore, his [Perry's] suite of officers formed a double line along the landing place, and as he passed up between, they fell into order behind him. . . . The United States flag and the broad pennant were borne by two athletic seamen, who had been selected from the crews of the squadron on account of their stalwart [large] proportions. Two boys, dressed for the ceremony, preceded the Commodore, bearing in an envelope of scarlet cloth the boxes which contained his credentials and the President's letter. These documents . . . were beautifully written on vellum, and . . . bound in blue silk velvet. Each seal, attached by cords of interwoven gold and silk with pendent [hanging] gold tassels, was encased in a circular box . . . wrought of pure gold. Each of the documents, together with its seal, was placed in a box of rosewood . . . , with lock, hinges, and mountings all of gold. On either side of the Commodore marched a . . . personal guard . . . two of the best looking fellows . . . the squadron could furnish. All this, of course, was but for effect."

—*Francis L. Hawks, a member of Perry's team, 1853*

next. Opinion was divided. Some daimyo were cautiously willing to open ports and allow some trade. They argued that Japan had to buy time to modernize its military to avoid a fate similar to the foreigners' incursions into China. Other daimyo wanted to fight rather than permit any contact with the foreigners. Some daimyo criticized the shogunate for betraying the nation by showing weakness in the face of the foreign threat. A number of important daimyo and scholars felt that only in the name of the emperor, Japan's rightful ruler, could the nation rally against the intruders.

## ANSWERING THE UNITED STATES

In dealing with Perry, the Japanese were not operating in a vacuum. They may have been stunned by the appearance of Perry's dark-hulled, smoke-belching black ships. But Japanese leaders knew more about the United States than the Americans knew about Japan, thanks to Dutch sources at Deshima and a handful of Japanese with foreign experience. The Japanese leadership knew about the Mexican-American War, in which the United States had expanded its territory all the way to California. Expedition artist William Heine recalled Japanese officials who, when shown a world map, "asked a variety of questions, indicating considerable knowledge of international affairs. . . . 'Does Mexico still exist? Or has the United States conquered it by now?'. . . With each [question], a finger went—correctly—to the place meant."

Japanese leaders knew the United States would probably use force if their demands were rejected. They knew Japan's defenses were outdated and weak. If no agreement were made, then the Americans—or the British soon after them—would enter Japan at will.

Senior councillors desperately tried to prepare a response that minimally accepted the United States' conditions. When Perry returned with his reinforced squadron in February 1854, the Japanese pleaded that Japan had been preoccupied by the recent death of shogun Ieyoshi and that the new shogun, Iesada, could not in any case change the exclusion laws. The Japanese even promised to provision ships and aid shipwrecked sailors. Perry was appreciative, but he wanted a genuine treaty, with no more excuses. If no treaty were forthcoming, Perry stated that he would send for a much larger force from the United States, whose mission might not be peaceful.

Perry's threats soon paid off, and the two sides negotiated seriously. Most U.S. demands were addressed in the agreement that emerged, known as the Treaty of Kanagawa, signed on March 31, 1854. Under the treaty, the ports of Shimoda, about 80 miles (130 kilometers) southwest of Tokyo, and Hakodate (in Hokkaido) would be opened to U.S.

Moryamo Yenoski (left) and Tako Juro (right) represented Ieseda in talks with Perry.

ships for provisioning (supplies). U.S. ships could use other ports but only in emergencies. A diplomatic representative from the United States would be assigned to Shimoda. Shipwrecked U.S. sailors would be helped, not mistreated. The treaty also stated that the United Sates would not interfere in Japanese religious matters, addressing old Japanese fears. Perry, aware of Japanese opposition, did not press to include provisions on trade.

The treaty was signed on March 31, 1854, amidst great ceremony. The Japanese treated the Americans to a Japanese wrestling match and gave out farewell presents. The

*Perry's officers watch a Japanese wrestling match after the signing of the Treaty of Kanagawa in 1854. The image comes from a scroll made in 1906 by a Japanese artist.*

Americans entertained the Japanese with a musical review and presented gifts for Japanese officials and the emperor.

While sword-bearing samurai delighted in riding on a miniature railway that the United States had given Japan as a gift, the Americans prepared to leave. Both parties could congratulate themselves. The Americans had fulfilled their goal of a direct treaty with Japan that allowed for provisioning ships, caring for shipwrecked sailors, and U.S. representation. The Japanese had at least limited the Americans to two ports, kept them a safe distance from Edo, and sidestepped the crucial issue of trade.

Perry returned home to great acclaim. The Japanese braced for a foreign onslaught. The United States may have seemed less threatening than other powers. Some believed a U.S. treaty—however difficult to swallow—could protect Japan from being forced to accept even worse arrangements. But the door was open, and other countries soon followed the U.S. lead. An armed British mission to Nagasaki in October of 1854 quickly forced similar terms from the Japanese. Treaties with France, Russia, and a stronger agreement with the Netherlands followed. Uneasy Japanese sensed the beginnings of great changes.

## JAPANESE REACTION TO THE TREATY

Young samurai raged at shogunate weakness in approving the U.S. treaty and began plotting against it. The shogunate itself took belated steps to modernize its military forces and allow the daimyo to improve their defenses against the foreigners. Japan did not have a truly national military.

Many defense duties were traditionally assigned to the domains, while the shogunate defended areas under its direct control. It was painfully obvious that neither the shogunate nor the daimyo were prepared to resist modern military forces. Frantic efforts to update and strengthen Japan's defenses began.

Perry's visit had opened other doors that would be hard to shut. By consulting with the daimyo on how to respond to Perry, Abe Masahiro had broken tradition and shaken up old ideas on how decisions were made and who could make them. Daimyo of domains loyal to the Tokugawas were upset that Abe had also consulted untrustworthy outer domains long excluded from shogunate affairs.

The experienced and moderate Hotta Masayoshi, soon replaced Abe as leader of the senior councillors. Japan bought some modern weapons and steam vessels from the Dutch. Hotta placed the responsibility for Japan's defense in the hands of a leader named Tokugawa Nariaki.

Nariaki was the former daimyo of Mito and was the leading spokesperson for a growing movement called *sonno joi*. The phrase means "revere the emperor and expel the barbarians." Increasing numbers of young samurai, particularly in the southwest, were inspired by this rallying cry. Its message was that to overcome the dangers from foreigners, a new Japan had to be reborn in the name of the emperor. The call for change was widely heard, especially among the lower and middle ranks of samurai. True patriotism meant restoring the emperor at the center of government in place of a shogun who was unworthy of holding power because he had yielded to the hated foreigners.

# THE HARRIS TREATY

Against this turbulent background the first U.S. consul (diplomatic representative), Townsend Harris, arrived in Shimoda. He took up his duties and pursued the unfinished business of a trade agreement. Harris proved to be as stubborn as Perry. He refused to remain isolated in Shimoda and insisted on presenting U.S. concerns in Edo. For two years, he pressured chief councillor Hotta on the need for a trade agreement. He was finally successful. The terms of the Treaty of Amity and Commerce (also known as the Harris Treaty) represented a much broader opening of Japan than the agreement with Perry.

*U.S. consul Townsend Harris, in a portrait taken about 1860*

According to the treaty, in 1859 Nagasaki and then Niigata would be opened to American shipping. Hyogo (Kobe) would be opened later. Americans could live and do business in Edo from 1862 on and Osaka from 1863. Opium could not be imported. Tariff terms (taxes on imports) would be fixed by agreement. Americans' crimes in Japan could only be tried in U.S. consular courts, not in Japanese courts.

The last two provisions were key features of the unequal treaties that had become infamous in Western dealings with Asia. These terms meant that the Americans could demand low tariffs, which favored U.S. businesses over their Japanese competitors. Particularly insulting was extraterritoriality, the principle that foreigners suspected of crimes could be tried only in foreign-run—not Japanese—courts. The Harris Treaty, like many other unequal treaties negotiated by Western powers throughout Asia, took the view that Japan's laws were unpredictable and barbarous and Americans should not be subject to such laws. The effect was to allow foreigners to behave as they pleased toward the Japanese without fear of answering for it in Japanese courts.

Hotta Masayoshi, the chief councillor, took the unprecedented step of making a formal visit to the emperor in Kyoto to request approval of the Harris Treaty. The move backfired badly. The Emperor Komei, living in isolated splendor in his palace, hated foreigners, even though he had never met one. He rejected the treaty, instead of rubber-stamping it as Hotta had expected. After consulting with the daimyo and the senior Tokugawa leadership, Hotta again attempted to get approval and again was put off. The imperial court's sudden assertion of authority was a shock.

Hotta Masayoshi had shamed the shogunate and had to resign as chief councillor. His role was taken over by a powerful daimyo named Ii Naosuke. Ii also was in favor of making a deal with the Americans. He sincerely believed that Japan's survival depended on accommodating the foreign powers until Japan was prepared to stand up to them. Many Japanese leaders found such a policy deeply distasteful and opposed it. Unlike Hotta, Ii moved to strengthen the shogunate and crush the opponents of this treaty.

In July 1858, Ii signed the Harris Treaty on behalf of

the shogunate, ignoring imperial disapproval and without waiting for further consultations with the daimyo. More treaties with foreign powers would follow.

## A NEW SHOGUN

Adding to the tension was a crisis over who would succeed the dying shogun Iesada. Many daimyo supported Tokugawa Yoshinobu for the position. His father had issued the call to "expel the barbarians, revere the Emperor" inspiring the sonno joi movement. But Ii Naosuke did not want antiforeign passions upsetting his precarious dealings with the foreign powers. He supported a much younger and more easily controlled candidate, Tokugawa Yoshitomi. Yoshitomi won.

The new shogun, who took the name Iemochi, was barely a teenager. So Ii would continue to run Japan and could proceed with what he saw as his duty. This involved the distasteful but necessary task of opening and modernizing the country so that Japan could eventually resist the power of the West. Ii worked for an arranged marriage between the emperor's sister, Princess Kazunomiya, and Shogun Iemochi. He hoped this would link the imperial court in Kyoto with the shogunate.

Ii dealt swiftly with opposition to his treaty decisions and moved to silence the leading antishogun voices. Some were stripped of their positions. Many pro-emperor samurai were jailed or executed. These measures came too late. The swelling antiforeign, pro-emperor movement was becoming radically antishogunate. Ii Naosuke would not long stand in the way. Like many Japanese leaders in the coming years, Ii would pay for his politics with his life.

# CHAPTER FOUR

# VIOLENT REACTIONS

The head of the Regent [Ii] is said to have been got safely
out of Yeddo [Edo], and presented to the Prince their master
who spat upon it . . . as the head of his greatest enemy. It was
then carried to . . . the capital of the Mikado [Kyoto, home of
the emperor] and there exposed at a place of execution . . .
and over it was placed a placard [sign], "This is the head of a
traitor who has violated the most sacred laws of Japan—those
which forbid the admission of foreigners into the country."

—British diplomat Rutherford Alcock, 1863

In March 1860, in San Francisco, California, the crew of
the *Kanrin Maru*—the first Japanese steamship to cross the
Pacific—is preparing to return to Japan. The first Japanese
diplomatic mission to the United States will soon be in
Washington, D.C., to witness the ratification (approval) of the
Harris Treaty, the treaty that has brought Japan to the boiling
point. The kimono-clad Japanese envoys—exotic to the eyes
of Americans, dignified, armed with their samurai swords—

Ambassadors from Japan arrive in Washington, D.C., for the ratification of the Harris Treaty in 1860. The picture appeared in the New York magazine Harper's Weekly in May 1860.

will tour New York through cheering crowds. The poet Walt Whitman describes the scene in *The Errand-Bearers*:

> Over the western sea, hither from Niphon [Japan] come,
> Courteous, the swart [dark]-cheek'd two-sworded envoys,
> Leaning back in their open barouches [carriages],
>     bare-headed, impassive,
> Ride today through Manhattan.

Meanwhile, in Edo, seventeen young men from the Mito domain wait nervously near the massive Sakurada Gate of the shogun's castle, trying to keep warm as a light snow falls. The samurai from Mito could not forgive Ii Naosuke. Ii had punished and insulted the former lord of Mito, Tokugawa Nariaki, for his loyalty to the emperor. Nariaki had rallied support for the emperor's rejection of the Harris Treaty. Support for the emperor on this issue meant opposition to the shogun.

The shogunate had tried to silence critics of the treaty. Worse, it had tried to stop efforts to spread word of the emperor's opposition. Believing the shogunate was showing contemptible weakness to the foreigners and betraying the emperor, young swordsmen throughout Japan were turning to violence. Samurai in faraway Tosa domain had written a vow in their own blood to defend the imperial cause to the death.

It was Ii Naosuke's blood that would be shed first. The young Mito samurai watched as Ii's procession approached the gate. He was to meet with the teenager he had helped make shogun. Patriots who revered the emperor had to stop him.

These "men of spirit," or *shishi*, were also men of violent action. The samurai drew swords and rushed forward. They fought through the surprised guards and stabbed and hacked at Ii. They beheaded him in a final gesture of rage and contempt.

*Ii Naosuke, shown on a Japanese postcard from the 1920s*

Like modern terrorists, Ii's killers hoped to draw attention to their cause as they avenged injustices and insults. They felt that only bloodshed could resolve Japan's political tensions and usher in a new order. Many young samurai from the lower and middle ranks shared the views of Ii's killers. They had little to lose, lacking the larger incomes or positions in local governments that linked higher-rank samurai to the established order. In sonno joi hotbeds such as Kyoto, they mixed with *ronin*, masterless samurai. Many ronin, recently made rootless and dangerous, were eager to strike back at the shogunate for its insulting treatment of their former masters.

In the Mito domain, scholars had studied the history of Japan. Interest rose in Japanese studies promoting a kind of nativism—the view that Japan's history and culture were special and unique. The Mito school emphasized ancient Japanese traditions such as the gods and rites of the Shinto religion and the divine descent of the emperor. Their teachings encouraged a sense of nationhood centered on the emperor. They helped spread the idea that Japanese owed the emperor their highest loyalty—and that the shogun held office only by the grace of the emperor. Nativist teachers, such as Akita domain's Hirata Atsutane, inspired many followers.

Pro-emperor passions were inflamed when young samurai met together in swordsmanship schools. These schools and the urgings of nativist scholars to return to Japan's ancient traditions spread a kind of pro-emperor fundamentalism. Many young samurai became filled with spiritual and patriotic fervor. They believed it was their duty to expel the barbarians polluting the land of the gods and restore the emperor as the true head of the nation. They were politically inexperienced, impatient, self-righteous—and very dangerous.

The shogunate seemed paralyzed. It tried to hide Ii's murder, but news spread quickly. The assassins' deed found a receptive audience amid worries over foreign intentions, anger at the shogunate, and the rise of patriotic feeling centered on the emperor. Poems praising the sincerity and selflessness of Ii's killers circulated. Ii's killing signaled the beginning of a wave of threats and assassinations.

## LOYALTY AND PATRIOTISM

Crosscurrents of loyalty, anger, and hope flowed in many directions. Underlying the political drama were deep divisions over opening Japan to the West. The foreigners had to be kept from taking over Japan and destroying its soul. Still, to build Japan's defenses, it was necessary to master the military, scientific, and educational advances that had made Western societies such a powerful threat. Japan had to open up and modernize. The question was, on whose terms and under whose direction?

Traditionally, samurai owed absolute obedience to their daimyo, who provided their incomes and in whose name they fought. The daimyo, in turn, owed loyalty and obedience to the shogun. In principle, the unseen emperor granted each shogun his office. In practice, the Tokugawas controlled Japan from atop a pyramid of hereditary power relationships in which emperors did not interfere. The loyalties of many samurai were torn between their traditional obligations and an emerging crusade to restore the emperor to power.

In the decades before Perry, the legitimacy of the shogunate had already been challenged by some intellectuals. Restoring the authority of the emperor and reasserting the role of Shinto were concepts that were eagerly discussed among the educated. Also receptive were literate commoners, who had become more important as cities grew and the merchant class expanded.

Sonno joi extremists despised the shogunate for admitting the detested foreigners and for failing to consult the emperor and then ignoring his wishes. Since founding their shogunate, the Tokugawas had arrogantly acted as the rulers of Japan. Righting this centuries-old wrong and restoring the ancient powers of the emperor became the obsession of the young samurai who thirsted for action. The swordsmanship schools became hotbeds of sonno joi activity, including plotting shishi violence. Visionaries such as Yoshida Shoin of Choshu inspired followers who spread the pro-emperor message through their writings and teachings.

"While we were in London, a certain member of parliament sent us a copy of . . . a protest against the arrogant attitude of the British minister (ambassador) to Japan, Alcock, who had at times acted as if Japan were a country conquered by a military force. One of the instances mentioned . . . was that of Alcock's riding his horse into the sacred temple grounds of Shiba, an unpardonable insult to the Japanese."

—*Fukuzawa Yukichi, Japanese author and ambassador, 1898*

# BRAVING THE BLACK SHIPS: YOSHIDA SHOIN

Yoshida Shoin came from a modest samurai background. He inspired the radicals who became convinced that the answer to Japan's problems was to restore imperial rule.

Influenced by scholars who saw Japan in a race to modernize before being overwhelmed by the Western powers, Shoin thirsted to know more of the outside world. He studied modern military tactics and secretly visited the Dutch outpost of Deshima. His wanderings convinced him that only modernizing under the emperor could prevent a foreign takeover. For leaving his domain without permission, Shoin's lord stripped him of his samurai status—but supported him in his continuing studies.

To Shoin, the arrival of Perry's "black ships" brought the foreign threat to the heart of Japan. Desperate to learn about Western ways in order to build a strong Japan, Shoin and a friend boarded one of Perry's ships at night and begged the sailors to let them leave with the Americans. The Americans, anxious not to offend the shogunate, rejected their pleas. Arrested, Shoin was harshly treated by the shogunate and then imprisoned in Choshu. In prison and when released under house arrest, Shoin continued to teach and promote modernization, improved military tactics, and emperor-centered patriotism. Shoin was executed in 1859 for involvement in an assassination plot against a shogunate official. He was twenty-nine years old.

"The Americans who arrived recently, though fully aware of the [shogunate's] prohibition, entered Uraga displaying a white flag as a symbol of peace and insisted on presenting their written requests. Moreover, they entered Edo Bay, fired heavy guns in salute and even went so far as to conduct surveys without permission. They were arrogant and discourteous, their actions an outrage. Indeed, this was the greatest disgrace we have suffered since the dawn of our history."

—*Tokugawa Nariaki*, Observations on Coastal Defense, *1854*

## DEATH TO THE FOREIGNERS

The first U.S.–Japan treaty had involved fairly limited U.S. demands. The Japanese had succeeded in keeping the Americans a safe distance from Edo, as well as putting off the issue of trade. The inrush of foreigners following the Harris Treaty alarmed many Japanese. The foreigners flooding in would do and take whatever they wanted.

Adding to the resentment against foreigners was an economic crisis caused by opening Japan to international trade. Silver was exchanged for gold in Japan at a ratio of five to one—that is, 5 ounces (142 grams) of silver would get you 1 ounce (28g) of gold. World trade at the time used a fifteen to one silver to gold ratio. Westerners needed 15 ounces (425g) of silver (three times as much) to get 1 ounce of gold. Since gold could be bought with much less silver in Japan, foreign merchants eagerly bought it. Gold drained

横濱渡來
亞墨利加
商人旅行
之圖

*Artist Utagawa Sadahide created a series of portraits of foreigners in Yokohama in the 1860s. This woodcut shows an American merchant walking with his daughter.*

out of Japan's economy. Inflation soared. High prices affected even basics such as rice. Poor harvests added to the crisis.

Westerners had strange customs. Even worse, they were disrespectful and highhanded in their dealings with local people. Thanks to the extraterritoriality clause in the treaties, foreigners felt they were beyond the reach of Japanese authorities and protested when officials tried to arrest them for offenses such as hunting or riding on farmland. To Japanese, used to the order of the Tokugawa centuries and the elaborate manners of a rigid social system, the ignorance and arrogance of the foreigners could be infuriating.

Other Western countries generally expected and received treaty conditions similar to the Harris Treaty. By 1859 foreigners had begun arriving in the ports designated by treaty. In the wide-open atmosphere of treaty ports such as Yokohama, adventurous young men out to make their fortunes and sailors from foreign ships wallowed in temptations. Drinking establishments were numerous. Prostitution was common. Brawls among foreigners were frequent occurrences. With shishi attacks a constant threat, many foreign residents carried arms.

In 1859 Yokohama saw its first killings of foreigners when some sailors were surprised from behind and hacked to death. There was no mistaking the attackers or their weapons. Only samurai swords could inflict such terrible wounds. Foreigners became prime targets throughout Japan. Killing them could help rally support for the sonno joi movement, frighten the foreigners into leaving, or start a war with the foreign powers. Many pro-emperor groups hoped for such a war. It could drive out the foreigners or further expose the shogunate's inability to protect Japan. Above all, the shishi wished to ease the mind of their revered emperor, whom they believed was deeply troubled by the growing foreign presence in Japan.

In January 1861, samurai from Satsuma ambushed and killed Townsend Harris's interpreter, Henry Heusken, as he rode back at night to the temple housing the U.S. legation. The young Dutchman enjoyed riding around Edo. To samurai—members of the only class privileged to be on horseback—he must have seemed an infuriating reminder of the growing foreign presence.

Heusken had been helping yet another foreign power, Prussia (part of present-day Germany), to force yet another treaty on Japan. His attackers may have associated him with the drama unfolding among the foreign powers, the shogunate, the daimyo, and the imperial court. It was a spiral of humiliation that drove the shishi to murder.

"Hewn down with the most ghastly wounds . . . left in a pool of blood, the flesh hanging in large masses from their bodies and limbs. The sailor was cleft [cut] through his skull to the nostrils, half the scalp sliced down, and one arm nearly severed from the shoulder through the joint. The officer was equally mangled, his lungs protruding from a saber gash across the body, the thighs and legs deeply gashed. The ruffians, it appears, were not content with simply killing, but must have taken pleasure in cutting them to pieces."

—Rutherford Alcock, describing an attack on Russian sailors, 1860s

With the door forced open by the major powers, the shogunate had to negotiate treaties with even minor Western nations. Meanwhile, the imperial court and pro-emperor daimyo were becoming more opposed to the treaties and more in favor of expelling all foreigners. The shogunate was forced to give the appearance of trying to expel the foreigners, even though this risked war with the treaty powers. The shogunate leadership promised, delayed, and bluffed.

The leaders had to endure being scolded and threatened by the foreign consuls, who held them responsible for protecting foreign residents, tracking down and punishing murderers of foreigners, and even collecting payments for indemnities (damages) from the domains of the murderers. Promising expulsion of the foreigners while actually delaying it made the shogun leadership look insincere and fueled the radicals' hatred. Resisting foreign demands only intensified foreign pressure. In the coming years, the shogunate would repeatedly find itself in this impossible position.

On a July night in 1861, samurai assailants stormed the British legation in Edo and were repulsed after a brisk fight. Mito samurai were blamed. The British were quick to demand reparations, punishment for the guilty, and improvements in the legation's defenses. The legation attack was one more sign of a rising tide of xenophobia—fear and hatred of foreigners.

In the summer of 1862, a samurai supposedly protecting the British legation killed two guards. In February 1863, the legation building was burned down by a group of Choshu samurai that included future leaders of Japan.

An assassination attempt early in 1862 had badly wounded Ando Nobumasa, head of the shogunal government after Ii's death. Ando had continued Ii's policies of crushing opposition and attempting to unite emperor and shogunate by the shogun's marriage to Princess Kazunomiya. The attackers also resented Ando's role in punishing imperial court nobles who opposed him.

No one was immune. Assassins' targets included anyone connected with the treaties opening Japan or working against the pro-emperor cause. Victims' heads were often displayed publicly along with warnings. In 1862 it was the turn of Shimada Sakon, a court noble who had helped arrange the royal marriage, supported Ii on the Harris Treaty, and identified antishogunate nobles whom Ii had punished. His severed head was found by a bridge in Kyoto next to a message: "This was what happened to a traitor."

# CHAPTER FIVE
# ON THE BRINK

Poor Richardson's corpse was found under the shade of a tree by roadside. His throat had been cut as he was lying there wounded and helpless. The body was covered by sword cuts, any one of which was sufficient to cause death.

—*Ernest Satow, describing the murder of a British businessman by samurai guards, 1862*

It was a splendid day for a ride—a bit of sightseeing, a break from the confines of Yokohama's foreign enclave. What started out as a lark for visiting British businessman Charles Richardson and three British friends soon turned into a nightmare. On the great Tokaido highway linking Edo with Kyoto, they met the procession of one of Japan's most powerful men, Shimazu Hisamitsu, returning to his Satsuma domain.

*Travelers walk along the Tokaido highway. Felice Beato, a British citizen who was one of the first photographers to visit Japan, captured this scene in about 1865.*

In Edo, Hisamitsu had been helping convince the shogun's government to cooperate more closely with the imperial court. His Satsuma samurai had been in the thick of antiforeign agitation. They were not the kind of men to tolerate the rude customs of foreigners. The British riders approached too close to the palanquin (a covered chair carried by several people) of Lord Shimazu, ignoring the shouts and gestures of his guards. While Japanese customarily greeted a mighty lord's procession by kneeling in a low bow and averting their eyes lest they become instant victims of "slaying for rudeness," the foreigners kept riding.

Warnings may have been exchanged, but neither party understood the other. The final provocation may have been when Richardson struck a samurai with his whip. Or perhaps it was the mere act of Richardson turning his horse toward Hisamitsu's palanquin. Whatever the insult, a Shimazu samurai drew his sword and slashed at the Englishman. Richardson galloped off but collapsed near a roadside inn, where other samurai found and killed him. The two other Englishmen were badly wounded.

The remaining rider—a young Englishwoman—rode unhurt back to Yokohama, where her news provoked a furious foreign reaction. The British representative in Yokohama convinced angry Westerners not to go after the

*This Japanese wood-block print from the late 1800s shows Shimazu samurai attacking Charles Richardson's party on the Tokaido highway.*

procession. Negotiations had to precede military action, even though the Japanese had violated treaty obligations that ensured freedom of movement near the treaty ports and guarantees for the safety of foreigners.

## BRITAIN VS. SATSUMA

Although Richardson's killers had been samurai from the Satsuma domain, the British held the shogunate responsible as the government of Japan. The British also demanded that Satsuma apologize, pay a large indemnity, and hand over the guilty samurai. But the daimyo of Satsuma would not cooperate. The Satsuma response was evasive and defiant. No culprits could be found, Satsuma reported. And in any case, the insolent foreigners had only gotten what they deserved.

Samurai killing for showing disrespect was not a crime in Japan. In fact, such slayings for rudeness were a time-honored tradition for keeping the unarmed masses in fear of the warrior class. Westerners saw the incident as a barbaric attack on unarmed civilians and an example of the wave of antiforeign hate and violence that was sweeping Japan.

The shogunate was caught in the middle. Pressured by Britain, it was in the difficult position of giving in to foreign demands and trying to force its Satsuma vassal to surrender Richardson's killers for an almost certain death. If it refused, it faced war with Britain and probably other foreign powers as well. As the shogunate dithered and stalled for months, in March 1863, the emperor issued an order for the expulsion of all foreigners from Japan. The timing could not have been worse. The shogunate, forced to show loyalty to the imperial court, promised to obey. It delayed carrying out the expulsion order, arguing again that it needed to first build up its military capabilities.

Satsuma continued its defiance. The shogunate begged the British for more time and understanding. But the British had had enough. An example would be made. After a final warning, the British informed the shogunate that they would proceed with a military solution. The Royal Navy would pay Satsuma a visit.

In mid-August 1863, a British fleet entered Kagoshima Bay. The British gave Satsuma officials a last chance to meet their demands, but they only met with more evasion. The defiant Satsuma blamed the shogunate and its despised treaties for not keeping foreigners from interfering with a daimyo's procession.

Last-minute negotiations proved useless. The British proceeded to seize, plunder, and burn some foreign-built Satsuma steamships. Satsuma's shore-based artillery (large guns) replied, and the fight was on. Young British diplomat Ernest Satow recalled how, in a driving rain, the British fleet bombarded the city and forts of Kagoshima "at a distance of about 400 yards [400 m] each vessel as she passed pouring her broadsides into the successive forts." British rockets fired into Kagoshima set fire to the town.

After more bombardment of the shore and lively Japanese return fire, the British left. Satsuma claimed success in repelling the attackers. But it quickly paid the indemnity, acknowledged Satsuma's wrongdoing, and promised to deliver Richardson's killers. (The killers were never found.)

# TOGO AT KAGOSHIMA

Heihachiro Togo, a fifteen-year-old samurai, worked furiously with his gun crew in August 1863, firing back at British ships bombarding Kagoshima as punishment for the Richardson affair. The hot action that day was Togo's baptism of fire. Claimed as a Satsuma victory, the battle showed the value of the domain's military modernization program. Young Togo joined the new Satsuma navy—a vital part of the pro-emperor forces—and fought in the naval battles of the restoration of the emperor. Later, he learned the skills of a modern naval officer while studying in Britain among his former enemies. Togo was involved in the building of Japan's modern navy and took an active part in imperial Japan's expeditions and wars. For his bold and decisive leadership of Japanese naval forces in the Russo-Japanese War (1904–1905), Togo became a national hero.

*Heihachiro Togo became commander-in-chief of the Japanese navy in 1903.*

To the surprise of the British, Satsuma officials seemed to show no ill feelings. They requested British help in obtaining a modern warship. This began a close relationship between Satsuma and Great Britain.

"And it is not a little remarkable that neither the Satsuma nor the Choshu men ever seemed to cherish any resentment against us for what we had done, and during the years of disturbance and revolution that followed they were always our most intimate allies."

—Ernest Satow, British diplomat, 1921

## THUNDER IN THE STRAITS

Another incident brought Japanese-Western relations to a boil. Choshu—a large and important domain at the southwestern tip of Kyushu—was another hotbed of antiforeign, pro-emperor sentiment. Like Satsuma, Choshu was far from the center of Tokugawa power in Edo. Also like Satsuma, the family of Choshu's daimyo had been on the losing side against Tokugawa Ieyasu in 1600. They had seen their domains reduced and had been excluded from the inner leadership of the shogunate government. Choshu was also one of the most militarily advanced domains, and it had been arming itself with modern weapons.

Choshu controlled some strategic territory—the

Shimonoseki Straits between Kyushu and Honshu. Vessels going from eastern Japan to China and Korea or to the Japanese coast along the Sea of Japan had to pass through the narrow straits. The Choshu domain had fortified the straits by placing artillery at key points. Foreign ships expected unchallenged passage through the waterway.

The emperor's expulsion edict had required the shogunate to reverse policies it had struggled to shape. The shogunate had sworn obedience, stalled, and promised action when forces were ready. Among sonno joi advocates, however, patience with the foreigners and with the shogunate's stalling was at an end. The emperor's expulsion edict had inspired a Choshu escalation of violence.

# THE RETURN OF THE STOWAWAYS

Just as hostilities were about to break out with the allied powers at Shimonoseki, two young Choshu samurai, former students of Yoshida Shoin, returned from the West. They were part of a group that had smuggled themselves aboard foreign ships and gone to Britain to learn the secrets of the West's strength. They had experienced firsthand British education, social institutions, and industries. On their return to Japan in 1864, they desperately tried to tell anyone in Choshu who would listen, "Don't fight the Westerners; Learn from them." It was too late. Choshu received a bloody lesson about fighting the West before Japan was strong and unified.

In June and July of 1863, Choshu ships and artillery had attacked U.S., French, and Dutch vessels in the Shimonoseki Straits. A U.S. warship, the USS *Wyoming*, had retaliated by sinking or damaging Choshu warships. A French expedition bombarded a Choshu town and destroyed artillery positions. The threat of Choshu shelling, however, kept foreign vessels from using the straits. Warnings, attempts to negotiate, and shows of force by the foreign powers failed to reopen them.

The shogunate government seemed helpless to prevent Choshu's continued attacks on shipping. It was once more time for direct Western action. In August 1864, an allied expedition including British, Dutch, and French warships and one U.S. vessel gathered at Yokohama. They were watched by a shogunate perhaps secretly pleased at

*British, Dutch, and French warships attack Choshu forces in 1864. French artist Jean Baptiste Henri Durand-Brager created this oil painting about 1865.*

this foreign punishment of a difficult vassal. The fleet of eighteen vessels, carrying thousands of soldiers and marines, proceeded to the Shimonoseki Straits. After massive bombardments on September 5 and 6, allied forces landed to destroy Choshu artillery. Fighting with Choshu forces produced more casualties, mainly Japanese. Choshu, whose forces stopped fighting on September 8, had learned a painful lesson in Western military superiority.

Negotiations produced an agreement that opened the straits. The Western powers demanded a large cash indemnity from Choshu. The shogunate felt forced to cover it. The shogunate's difficulties in paying would give the Westerners—confident after their success at Shimonoseki—more leverage to force demands on it. These demands made the shogunate seem even weaker to imperial loyalists and further inflamed shishi hatred and contempt.

# CHAPTER SIX

# JAPAN IN CRISIS

Alas! Wherever you look . . . , you will see that the dangers threatening us are great and imminent indeed. At home, the scene is virtually one of disintegration and collapse: public order has broken down, high and low are disunited, and the people suffer great extremes of distress. Abroad, we are subjected to the insults of five arrogant powers; conquest by them seems certain to be our fate. Thinking of this, I can neither sleep by night nor yet swallow food.

—*Emperor Komei to Shogun Iemochi,*
*during the shogun's visit to Kyoto, 1864*

The mid-1860s were exciting but uncertain times in Japan. Loyalties were tested and reaffirmed, broken and recast. Samurai from domains such as Aizu with a strong relationship to the shogunate would serve their daimyo loyally to the end. Young shishi radicals from domains such as Choshu were becoming the shock troops of the antishogun movement, willingly serving daimyo they felt were pro-emperor.

Pro-emperor radicals were not simply a small minority of extremists alienated from the general population. Many Japanese appreciated their sincerity and intensity of purpose. They saw the radicals as sincere patriots who could restore Japan to its former glory. A network of supporters arose. They helped radicals communicate with one another, move around Japan, and hide when necessary. The radicals' sympathizers included commoners and women.

Despite the many restrictions imposed on them by both law and tradition, many Japanese women found themselves inspired by the patriotic feelings sweeping Japan and did what they could to help the sonno joi cause. Stories of the period tell of young women hiding radicals, warning them, or helping them escape from shogun authorities. Some degree of literacy was not unusual among women, even from households of modest means and social standing. Families that could afford to educate their daughters usually did so. Educated women followed the intellectual currents and events of the day. Many found themselves drawn to the cause of restoring the emperor.

This wood-block print from the late 1800s shows a woman in traditional clothing.

# MATSUO TASEKO

Matsuo Taseko (1811–1894) was born into the highest reaches of the peasant class. No stranger to hard work on her family's land, she was also well educated and interested in intellectual pursuits.

Married at seventeen into a family of somewhat higher rank, Taseko bore ten children, developed a profitable family silk-culture business, and still found time to travel central Japan with her husband. She absorbed the teachings of Hirata Atsutane and became known as an accomplished poet. Concerned by the prospect of Japan being polluted by foreigners, Taseko corresponded with thinkers and artists involved in the pro-emperor movement. She exchanged verses and letters with them and visited when she could. She helped bring together radicals and gave them aid and encouragement. For her support of the sonno joi movement, the Meiji government awarded her the title of a court noble after her death.

## THE STRUGGLE FOR POWER

At this time, Japanese internal politics took center stage. The shogunate was clearly in trouble. In the ten years since the Perry treaty, the shogunate's strength and confidence had declined. In contrast, the growing strength of the pro-emperor movement was creating a state of near rebellion among some daimyo and samurai. The imperial court in Kyoto was becoming increasingly stubborn in its opposition to the foreign presence. Both the emperor's court and the daimyo were getting used to asserting themselves against the shogunate—something that had not happened in centuries.

Since the early 1860s, the shogunate had been under increasing pressure from powerful daimyo to reverse its policies. There had been ominous signs and threats that the well-armed and well-organized domains of the southwest might turn on them and support the wishes of the imperial court. In 1862 the powerful lord Shimazu Hisamitsu of Satsuma had moved north with Satsuma troops—hotheaded samurai eager to support the imperial cause. Satsuma samurai then escorted an imperial court noble to the shogunate in Edo to back up the message that the emperor wanted the foreigners out. This threat of court-daimyo cooperation helped convince the shogunate to appoint a new chief councillor who could work with the court and the daimyo. An important daimyo and a Tokugawa relative, Matsudaira Shungaku avoided the heavy-handed tactics of previous chief councillors. However, those who hoped the shogunate would get serious about expelling the foreigners and honoring the emperor would be bitterly disappointed.

Matsudaira Shungaku ruled his family's domain until 1858. He became chief councillor of the shogunate in 1862.

Pressure from court and daimyo, maneuvering by Councillor Shungaku, and assassination threats against key shogunal leaders brought Tokugawa Yoshinobu back into national politics as guardian to the teenage shogun Iemochi. Yoshinobu was the son of the former daimyo of Mito. He had been adopted into a branch of the Tokugawa family from which shoguns were traditionally chosen. With his maturity and training, he had been a strong candidate to become shogun in 1858. The young and easily manipulated Iemochi had been chosen instead, while Yoshinobu's antiforeign father had been arrested and stripped of his position. Yoshinobu found himself out of favor with the shogunate.

Shungaku and Yoshinobu tried to revitalize the shogunate through new policies. Against strong opposition, Shungaku arranged an amnesty, forgiving those who had been punished earlier for political crimes and even assassinations. But it was not enough to save the shogunate.

## THE FOREIGN QUESTION

By the mid-1800s, the question of expelling the foreigners was convulsing Japanese politics. Alliances and positions shifted and swirled around the issue, and motives and plans were rarely transparent. The shogunate, in particular, seemed to be playing a double game. It was committed by its treaties to a schedule of opening certain ports to foreigners even as it claimed to honor the emperor's wishes for expulsion. Emperor Komei had demanded the immediate closing of the ports already open, though important daimyo joined with the shogunate to convince him that expelling foreigners should be accomplished through negotiation rather than violence.

Among the lords who took a strong position against hastily closing ports was Shimazu Hisamitsu of Satsuma. He had learned a harsh lesson in Western power when the British bombarded his domain. Originally the shogunate had opposed any actions, like port closing, that might look anti-Western. However, in order to demonstrate its new closeness to the court, the shogunate had to appear to favor closing the ports. It was hard for daimyo and their retainers to know whose side and whose positions could be trusted.

While the shogunate tried to maintain its hold on power as it dealt with the troublesome foreigners, most of the political action shifted to Kyoto. Dealing with the daimyo, keeping alive the improved relations between imperial court and shogunate, and countering radical plots against it became major concerns of Yoshinobu. These problems kept him in Kyoto much of the time. In addition to the daimyo and shogunal officials, new players emerged from among the imperial court nobles. Some became spokespersons for the imperial cause, while others actively conspired with radicals—mainly from Choshu.

Restless young samurai were also drawn to the imperial capital. Many were from the lower ranks. Some owned little more than their swords. Some were ronin disowned by their daimyo or whose pro-emperor lords had been forced from office. Others were troublemakers on the run from shogunate police. The unseen emperor's presence made Kyoto the focus of powerful religious and nationalist feelings. The political passions of the young shishi samurai often spilled

*Three samurai wearing traditional armor and carrying traditional weapons pose for a portrait. The picture was taken in the mid-1800s.*

over into violence. Even though the shogunate had promised to respect the emperor's expulsion edict, its inaction and seeming insincerity, along with continuing foreign arrogance, left the shishi itching for a fight.

Matsudaira Katamori, daimyo of Aizu domain, reluctantly accepted the office of protector of Kyoto to maintain order and defend the shogunate's interests there. Katamori used troops from Aizu and other domains as well as a special policing unit called the *shinsengumi*.

# SHINSENGUMI

The shogunate employed a group of ronin, the *shinsengumi*, to help police Kyoto. In their distinctive blue-and-white uniforms, these young swordsmen developed a reputation for ferocity as they eliminated the shogun's opponents. The shinsengumi were among the last forces to stand with the shogunate.

*Kondo Isami became a shinsengumi commander in 1863.*

The ruthlessness, finely honed fighting skills, and group loyalty of the colorful shinsengumi continue to fascinate modern Japanese. The shinsengumi have been widely portrayed in Japanese *manga* (comics), anime (animated stories), video games, films, and television dramas set in the last turbulent days of the shoguns.

## GOING TO KYOTO

Nothing had symbolized the shifts in Japanese politics as clearly as the shogun's visit to Kyoto. Shungaku arranged for the shogun to visit Kyoto in the spring of 1863. This kind of visit had occurred only once before under the Tokugawas, in 1634. Then an all-powerful shogun had called on a powerless emperor. This time it seemed it was the shogun who would pay homage to the emperor in Kyoto.

As a first item of business in Kyoto, Yoshinobu, representing the young shogun, had felt it necessary to formally request that the emperor confirm the shogun's authority. The emperor maintained the shogun in his powers but ordered him to cooperate with the daimyo and to expel the barbarians. The once-secluded and powerless emperor gave orders to the Tokugawas, who had held Japan in an iron grip for 250 years. The tide had indeed turned.

Amid this uncertainty and the weakness of shogunal authority, sonno joi radicals from Choshu became bolder. Simmering plots erupted into an attempted takeover of the Imperial Palace. The radicals had to be driven from Kyoto by Aizu and Satsuma forces loyal to the shogunate.

## 1864—THE SHOGUNATE HOLDS ON

The shogun again visited Kyoto in early 1864. The imperial court approved the shogunal approach of cautiously handling foreign expulsion through negotiation. The shogunate, in turn, appeared to firmly commit itself to expulsion, even though most shogunate leaders and many daimyo knew the foreigners would defend their treaty rights with war. Stalling on treaty obligations only gave foreign powers an excuse to press for even more concessions. This inflamed the radicals' hatred of foreigners and the seemingly spineless shogunate. Pro-emperor feeling grew stronger.

As the *kobu-gattai* ("union of court and shogunate") movement and the marriage of Iemochi to the emperor's sister seemed to bring the shogun and emperor closer, the great lords felt excluded from important decisions. Back in their domains, some daimyo found themselves forced to crack down on shishi radicals who were causing unrest. Some daimyo hesitated to take sides. They wondered if the shogunate could actually hold on to power. The shogunal government's own vassals were slow to crush an uprising of Mito samurai dangerously near Edo.

Shishi rage finally boiled over. In the summer of 1864, a large group of Choshu radicals marched on Kyoto in another attempt to seize the Imperial Palace. As with a smaller-scale coup (overthrow) attempt in 1863, this armed raid was smashed by Aizu and Satsuma forces and other groups loyal to the shogunate. The Choshu rebels were driven from the city. Court nobles involved in the coup attempt fled with them to Choshu. Kyoto suffered major damage from fires started in the battle. An angry imperial court demanded that the shogunate punish Choshu.

*Shishi radicals fight at the Hamaguri Gate of the Imperial Palace in Kyoto in 1864. Japanese artist Mori Yuzan created this woodcut around 1893.*

With its prestige enhanced by its new closeness with the court, the shogunate commanded its vassals to gather for war against Choshu. Then more moderate leaders seized power in Choshu. Negotiations with the new leaders defused the crisis. Key radical leaders were executed or required to commit suicide. But skillful negotiations helped Choshu and its ruling family avoid the worst. The Choshu domain could easily have been greatly reduced in size or had its ruling family replaced, the traditional shogunate treatment of rebellious domains. The scheming court nobles were exiled rather than executed.

The shogunate pressed its luck and tried to reassert its old power. Daimyo were informed that required attendance in Edo would be resumed. Few obeyed. In an atmosphere of growing violence and uncertainty, daimyo were not about to risk offering their families and themselves as hostages in Edo. The imperial court intervened. It supported the lords' complaint that their limited funds were needed for defense, not expensive stays in Edo. All too aware of its own weakening authority, the shogunate gave up and turned to more urgent problems.

## CITIES AND DOMAINS

Edo was a place of rumor, anxiety, and fear. The city must have seemed half empty with the end of the forced attendance. The presence of foreigners, foreign fleets, and foreign troops at nearby Yokohama added to the tension.

The shogunate made an effort to reform its shaky finances. It employed a French military mission to modernize and train shogunal forces. The French minister

*People of several nations eat, play, and converse with Japanese visitors at a house set aside for foreigners in Yokohama. A Japanese printmaker made this image in the early 1860s.*

Leon Roche was one foreign representative who believed the shogunate would survive. The focus of power, though, was no longer in Edo.

Intense power struggles in Kyoto swirled around the emperor secluded in his palace. They were fueled by the violent ambitions of those who hoped to speak for the emperor and act in his name. A commoner in Kyoto could only marvel at the grand processions of daimyo and even the shogun arriving on affairs of state. The mighty of the land were eager to learn the emperor's will.

Kyoto's people knew fear too. A sophisticated backwater while Japan was ruled from Edo, Kyoto became the place to be. For many, it was a very dangerous place. The city filled with rumors, plots and counterplots, and armed, surly young

men ready for trouble. Shishi were involved in street brawls and assassinations. The shogunate ruthlessly hunted down troublemakers and broke up plots. Pitched battles were fought within the city. Entire neighborhoods burned.

In nearby Osaka, worried merchants like those of the great house of Mitsui counted their gold and silver and checked their ledgers. Though commoners, they were linked to the samurai and daimyo through the time-honored cycle of lending them money until the rice harvests. The fortunes of the Osaka moneymen rose and fell with those of the daimyo and the samurai. As it became clear that many daimyo and samurai were rallying in support of the emperor, the Osaka business houses became an important source of financing for the imperial cause.

The cities experienced political and economic uncertainty. The fate of Japan came to rest with the domains of the southwest, principally Satsuma and Choshu, along with Tosa, Hizen, and others that had been out of favor with the Tokugawas. Satsuma and Choshu had in common large numbers of samurai (many of them pro-emperor), a tradition of independence from distant Edo, and an old grudge against the Tokugawas for defeating their domains and keeping them powerless since 1600. Satsuma, Choshu, and other domains such as Tosa were also relatively well-governed. They were among the most prosperous domains in Japan. This was in part due to economic reforms by capable daimyo. Satsuma, in particular, had benefited from profitable activities such as sugar growing and foreign trade through the Ryukyu Islands. The southwestern domains also could obtain modern foreign weapons from nearby Nagasaki.

At first, Satsuma and Choshu seemed destined to continue their old rivalry. Choshu had been a center of support for the emperor in his opposition to the treaties and a magnet for proimperial, antiforeign radicals. Satsuma had generally been more moderate. It had used its power to push the shogunate into closer cooperation with the emperor, helped force the shogunate to allow Yoshinobu to return to national affairs, and otherwise promoted the kobu-gattai movement on the side of the court. Satsuma helped the shogunate by suppressing radicals both within Satsuma and in Kyoto. Satsuma forces also had contributed to the 1864 expedition to crush radicals in Choshu.

# CHAPTER SEVEN

# THE END OF THE SHOGUNS

> If we decide to resort to arms, it can have the . . . effects of renewing the spirit of all people under heaven, and pacifying the central regions of the country. Therefore, we deem it the most urgent task to decide for war, and to find victory in the most difficult situation.
>
> —*Saigo Takamori and Okubo Toshimichi of Satsuma, 1867*

Despite the troubling rise of imperial and daimyo power and the growing realization that it could not always get its way, the shogunate had weathered 1864 fairly well. In 1865, however, things began falling apart. The catalyst was once again Choshu, where early in the year, pro-emperor radicals drove out the moderates in a second round of civil war. The shogunate again tried to mobilize vassals and build support for attacking and punishing the rebels. This time, however, its luck had run out.

The rebellion in Choshu signaled important new developments. Commoners were training and fighting alongside Choshu's samurai. They would more than prove themselves in the battles to come. The monopoly on violence that had been held by samurai for hundreds of years was broken. Choshu, along with Satsuma, already had a high percentage of samurai in its population. But arming the commoners added to the domain's fighting strength. The growing pro-emperor patriotism went beyond social class or domain loyalty.

The Choshu rebel forces were well armed. Nagasaki-based arms merchants found a welcome market as the southwestern domains modernized their forces along European lines. Choshu's and Satsuma's military buildups were well funded thanks to economic reforms. In 1865 a remarkable young ronin from Tosa, Sakamoto Ryoma, met with the emerging samurai leaders Saigo Takamori and Okubo Toshimichi of Satsuma and Ito Hirobumi and Kido

Sakamoto Ryoma, in a portrait taken in 1866

## SAKAMOTO RYOMA

Sakamoto Ryoma was a colorful, low-ranking samurai, who fled from Tosa and became a ronin. He helped to establish a modern naval academy in Hyogo and then worked to convince Satsuma and Choshu to cooperate secretly to defeat the shogunate. In June 1866, he wrote out an eight-part plan for the future of Japan while commanding a warship in the Shimonoseki Strait during the Summer War. He was thirty-three when he was assassinated in 1867.

Koin of Choshu to arrange a secret collaboration of these two well-armed and powerful domains that would grow into a powerful alliance. After the secret alliance was formed, Satsuma also began helping Choshu acquire arms.

## MORE FOREIGN TROUBLE

The year 1865 was not an easy one for shogunate-foreigner relations either. The Western powers used the shogunate's difficulties in paying the large cash indemnity owed for the Shimonoseki Straits Incident to pressure it to open ports. In September 1865, British, French, and Dutch warships anchored at Osaka. This threat so close to the imperial capital was coupled with an offer to reduce the indemnity in return for opening Osaka and Hyogo as soon as possible. To overcome antitreaty sentiment, the foreign powers also wanted the emperor to approve trade treaties previously signed by the shogunate.

After threats by Britain's minister, Harry Parkes, to attack

Kyoto itself, in October 1865, the emperor approved the treaties and the port openings. However, he quietly reminded the shogunate of the court's real intent of delaying, stopping, and eventually reversing port openings. In particular, Hyogo and Osaka were dangerously close to Kyoto and the imperial court.

Once more the shogunate was in an impossible position. While wanting to at least appear to respect the emperor's wishes for expulsion, it had to appear to the Westerners to be carrying out provisions of the treaties. Shogunate leaders were realistic. They knew that the opening of Japan could not be stopped, just managed. To keep its independence, Japan must modernize and join the larger world of international trade and politics. The shogunate, however, had to deal with the very different views of radicals, daimyo, and the imperial court.

## THE SHOGUNATE COLLAPSES

If 1865 had been bad for the shogunate, 1866 was far worse. As the rallying cry of reverence for the emperor was heard more widely in Japanese society, the shogunal government seemed to be losing its power. The shogun ordered the assembly of another expedition to punish the radicals in Choshu. Even with the support of the imperial court, daimyo responded slowly, half-heartedly, or not at all. Most disturbing, the Satsuma domain would not join in the expedition, honoring the secret agreement with Choshu arranged early in the year.

The shogunate gathered what forces it could and moved toward Choshu. The result was a disaster. In the Summer War of 1866, shogunate troops were badly defeated in efforts to punish the rebels in Choshu. Despite some local successes by modernized shogunal units, its military disorganization, poor leadership, shaky finances, and lack of daimyo support were painfully evident. Shogunate prestige seemed fatally damaged. The shogun Iemochi's death in July gave the battered shogunate an excuse to call for a truce, withdraw its forces, and consider its chances for survival.

The Summer War of 1866 was a terrible shock for the shogunate. With Iemochi's death, Yoshinobu became head of the Tokugawa house. He only reluctantly agreed to become shogun in January 1867. Perhaps he agonized over the shogunate's hopeless situation and his duty as a Tokugawa. The emperor approved the appointment.

The new shogun promised to govern virtuously and hoped to repair relations with the daimyo by including lords in national decision making. The shogunal government was frantically modernizing its military. Commoners were recruited to fight. Units were reorganized or dissolved. Swordsmen and pikemen (foot soldiers carrying long spears) took up modern rifles. Preparations were intensified for training under military advisers from France.

Attempting to raise desperately needed revenue through new forms of taxation, printing paper money, and negotiating foreign loans, the shogunate began modernizing its bureaucracy and centralizing some functions formerly performed by the domains. Plans were made to support economic development, employ foreign experts, and expand Western-style education and training. It was all to be too little, too late.

The Emperor Komei, the center of so much conflict and so

many hopes, died near the end of 1866. He was succeeded by his teenage son, Mutsuhito. History knows him by the name that was chosen for his reign, Meiji, or "Enlightened Rule"

## THE LAST DAYS OF THE SHOGUNATE

As if exhausted by the recent years of violence, political turmoil, economic chaos, and even poor harvests due to bad weather, Japan seemed quiet through the summer of 1867. The peace was broken only by *"ee ja nai ka,"* a kind of hysteria that swept parts of the country.

## PARTY AS THOUGH IT'S ALMOST YEAR ONE

One of the strangest aspects of the shogunate's final days was a nationwide outbreak of mass hysteria that began in June 1867. Shouting *"ee ja nai ka"* (Isn't it good?), crowds danced in the streets and good-naturedly entered homes and businesses. The party mood of a neighborhood festival mixed with religious excitement was inspired by the mysterious appearance of thousands of amulets (pieces of paper with prayers and charms written on them). The phenomenon seems to have been fueled by unease over Japan's troubles—severe inflation, fighting between the shogunate and pro-emperor domains, menacing foreigners—overlaid with wild hopes for great changes that were coming in a new age. In the months after the restoration of the emperor, the outbreak died down as mysteriously as it had begun.

The shogunate, reforms under way, even seemed to recover some of its strength after the Choshu disaster of 1866. Yoshinobu was finally able to get imperial approval to open Hyogo port to foreign trade. Hoping to calm the political situation, Yoshinobu met for talks with lords from several domains, including Shimazu Hisamitsu of Satsuma. The talks soon collapsed over well-founded suspicions that Satsuma planned to unite with Choshu in an attack on the shogunate.

A showdown between the pro-imperial southwestern domains and the shogunate looked inevitable. Sensing the end was near, Satsuma openly moved forces to Kyoto. (Choshu forces remained banned from the imperial capital for the earlier uprisings.) The Satsuma-Choshu alliance grew to include Tosa and other domains. As the southwestern domains massed their forces for an all-out civil war with the shogunate, a plan initiated by leaders from Tosa and supported by Satsuma was brought to the shogun. The plan proposed governing Japan through an assembly of daimyo and court nobles under the authority of the emperor. While Yoshinobu might retain a role as head of the substantial Tokugawa domains and hold high office in a new government, the plan meant the end of the Tokugawa shogunate.

Yoshinobu knew the shogunate's military weakness and took the plan seriously. Whatever improvements the year had seen, the shogunate's situation was grim. The growing power and confidence of the southwestern domains, now directed as much by radical pro-emperor samurai as by their domain lords, could not be ignored. Military preparations and political maneuvering by Satsuma and

Choshu were clearly aimed at attacking the shogunate. It seemed only a matter of time before antishogunate court nobles arranged for the young emperor to pardon Choshu and condemn the shogun.

Britain seemed to be siding with Satsuma and Choshu, and French help for the shogunate was slow in coming. Most important, Yoshinobu had an obligation to preserve the lands and positions of the Tokugawas. Even if he were not shogun, Yoshinobu expected to remain lord of the Tokugawa lands and to be a force in any new government.

Perhaps Yoshinobu was simply weary of trying to maintain his impossible position. By early November 1867, Yoshinobu had resigned as shogun, declaring that the peace and unity of the country required returning the shogunate's powers to the emperor. The family that had ruled Japan for more than two and a half centuries would rule no more.

The response to Yoshinobu's resignation was mixed. The emperor asked Yoshinobu to carry on governing with the advice of daimyo until

*Tokugawa Yoshinobu sought peace between the shogunate and the emperor.*

other arrangements could be made. Yoshinobu still headed the Tokugawa house with the forces of Tokugawa vassal domains at his command. Traditional loyalties died hard. Some fiercely loyal Tokugawa vassals wanted to attack anti-shogun forces immediately. Radical samurai leaders from Satsuma and Choshu schemed with court nobles to end Tokugawa power once and for all. They believed Japan could never unite if there was a chance of the Tokugawas reasserting their power or influencing the emperor.

Samurai from Satsuma and other pro-emperor domains took control of the Imperial Palace on January 3, 1868, in what amounted to a coup. Its leaders announced a decree by which the emperor restored to himself and his line all government powers. The decree eliminated most major positions in the shogunate—whose offices in theory had been still directing national affairs. The shogunate was no longer the national government of Japan. The country would be ruled by councillors drawn from the ranks of court nobles and from the domains involved in the coup.

## FINAL BATTLES

Lord Shimazu Hisamitsu of Satsuma opposed any Tokugawa participation in the new government as a threat to the new imperial order. The emperor had allowed the former shogun to remain in the government as an adviser. The new councillors from Satsuma and other victorious domains wanted none of that power sharing. They wanted Yoshinobu removed—by imperial decree or by force—not only from his position but from all his lands as well.

The emperors of Japan first took up residence in Kyoto in 794. The Imperial Palace, shown here in a 1910 picture, had been rebuilt and expanded several times before pro-emperor radicals seized it in 1868.

Yoshinobu and other shogunate leaders left Kyoto for Osaka, the Tokugawa stronghold in the region. The pro-emperor lords rightly saw themselves as winners and saw Yoshinobu as a man on the run. Protesting his treatment, Yoshinobu and his supporters sent troops to shore up the Tokugawa position in Kyoto. It was not a success, as the Tokugawa forces fell to a smaller attacking force from pro-emperor domains on January 25, 1868, at the Battle of Toba-Fushimi. Tokugawa hopes for a role in the new Japan were ended.

Within a week, Yoshinobu abandoned Osaka and sailed to Edo. Osaka fell to imperial forces a few days later. The emperor issued a decree that condemned Yoshinobu for continuing the fighting and ended his authority over

"There were warriors clad in the old armor of the country, carrying spears, bows and arrows, . . . with sword and dirk [short knife] . . . who looked as if they had stepped out of some old picture of . . . the Middle Ages. . . . Hideous masks of lacquer and iron, fringed with portentous [big, impressive] whiskers and moustachios, crested helmets with wigs from which long streamers of horsehair floated to their waists . . . the hobgoblins of a nightmare.

Soon a troop of horsemen appeared. The Japanese all prostrated themselves [lay down] and bent their heads in reverent awe. In the midst of the troop was the fallen prince . . . worn and dejected . . . his head wrapped in a black cloth, taking notice of nothing. . . . It was a wild and wonderful sight and one of the saddest I ever beheld. At the gate all dismounted —save only the War Lord himself—he rode in, a solitary horseman. It was the last entry of a Shogun into the grand old castle."

—A. B. Mitford, British diplomat, describing the retreat of the last shogun, Tokugawa Yoshinobu, into Osaka Castle

Tokugawa vassals. As imperial armies led by Satsuma's Saigo Takamori advanced north against little resistance. A truce was arranged. Yoshinobu gave up leadership of the Tokugawa house to a minor branch of the Tokugawas. Edo Castle was surrendered. Yoshinobu remained in Edo, his status uncertain.

Edo was occupied by imperial forces. Diehard Tokugawa supporters rose up in Edo in May 1868, in the Battle of Ueno—but were soundly defeated. Imperial armies moved toward the northeast, where loyal Tokugawa allies still resisted.

Tokugawa remnants fled to Hokkaido aboard shogunate navy vessels and declared themselves the Republic of Ezo. A group of French military advisers gallantly remained with the rebels, resigning from French service to do so. After an unsuccessful rebel attack against imperial ships at Miyako in northeast Honshu, imperial naval and land victories ended rebel resistance on Hokkaido in May 1869. The unimaginable had been accomplished. For the first time in seven centuries, Japan was truly unified under the emperor.

*Emperor Meiji in about 1883*

# CHAPTER EIGHT

# THE EMPEROR RESTORED

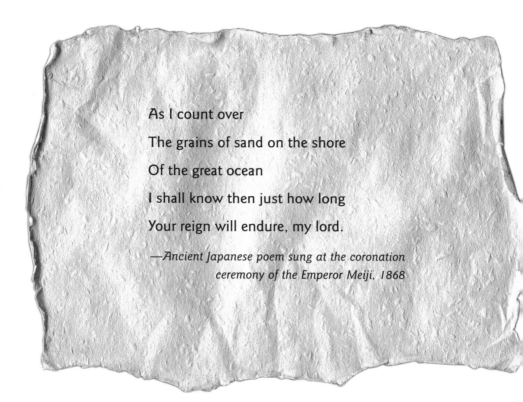

As I count over

The grains of sand on the shore

Of the great ocean

I shall know then just how long

Your reign will endure, my lord.

—*Ancient Japanese poem sung at the coronation*
*ceremony of the Emperor Meiji, 1868*

Emperors rarely explain themselves or their plans to those they rule. The new leaders advising the young Emperor Meiji, however, took the unusual step of issuing a statement in his name. Called the Charter Oath of 1868, it set out principles for Japan's new era. The Charter Oath was a sweeping and idealistic statement of the hopes of the leaders of the restoration of the emperor. It called for fundamental change and modernization.

*Emperor Meiji (at right, behind screens) listens as a minister reads the Charter Oath. This print appeared in Japan shortly after the new emperor took the throne in 1868.*

In the late autumn of 1868, a great procession left Kyoto and passed through central Japan. In November it arrived in Edo. The palanquin in the procession's center was carried into Edo Castle, the very heart of the former shogunate's power. The awestruck crowds fell silent and bowed in reverence. Inside the palanquin was young Emperor Meiji, freshly arrived in his new capital after having seen much of his realm for the first time.

By this oath we set up as our aim the establishment of the nation on a broad basis and the framing of a constitution and laws.

1. Deliberative assemblies shall be widely established and all matters decided by public discussion.

2. All classes, high and low, shall unite in vigorously carrying out the administration of affairs of state.

3. The common people, no less than the civil and military officials, shall each be allowed to pursue his own calling so that there may be no discontent.

4. Evil customs of the past shall be broken off and everything based upon the just laws of Nature.

5. Knowledge shall be sought throughout the world so as to strengthen the foundations of imperial rule.

—*The Charter Oath of 1868*

The emperor was to reside in Edo, the former city of the shogunate, which was renamed Tokyo, meaning "Eastern Capital." Moving the emperor from Kyoto—with its atmosphere of plots and intriguing court nobles—was one of many bold decisions made by an emerging group of leaders.

Many of the new leaders were lower- or middle-ranking samurai. Some had useful experience in domain administration. Many had risked their lives fighting against the shogunate. Satsuma and Choshu were heavily represented, along with Tosa, Hizen, and other southwestern domains. There was a sprinkling of court nobles too. All these men had proven themselves as practical and tough-minded leaders in the political struggles to restore the emperor.

Even though some had fought both the foreigners and the shogunate, few of the new leaders were rabid antiforeign extremists. It looked as if the day of the assassin and the xenophobe was over. The new leadership had come through the turmoil of the foreign threats and the shogunate's muddled response and downfall. But they had to establish more practical ways of dealing with the rest of the world. They needed new government structures and had to set in motion social and economic changes that would transform Japan.

## EXPERIMENTS WITH GOVERNMENT

In 1868 the practical challenges involved in establishing a new government for Japan seemed overwhelming. Politically, Japan was still more than 250 semi-independent domains. Previously, they had been united under feudal obligations and by the overwhelming power of the Tokugawas. Stability had been forced on the country by the shogunate, but that power was gone. The new government had to provide not only peace but the material and social progress that would enable Japan to take its place among the world's modern nations. The Japanese had to create for themselves unity, prosperity, and military power to be strong enough to resist continuing foreign threats.

In 1868 power belonged almost exclusively to the domain forces that had defeated the shogunate. These daimyo on the winning side—and the samurai who had been the backbone of the struggle—expected a voice in the new government. The Tokugawa leaders had governed through domain politics and consultation among senior vassals. The leaders of the Meiji Restoration called for something more.

They saw that the strongest of the foreign powers, such as Great Britain, had representative government. The leaders wanted to introduce it into Japan, but that was easier said than done. While the decisions of shoguns and daimyo had long involved consultation among senior advisers, the Japanese had no experience with representative government.

As a first step, the new leaders consulted with groups of senior and junior councillors appointed from different domains and from among court nobles and relatives of the emperor. The leaders produced a constitution based on the principles of the Charter Oath they had issued earlier in 1868. Despite the ideas about equality in the Charter Oath, people still thought of themselves as members of a particular class. Samurai, for example, were briefly given their own assembly to discuss traditional concerns that affected them, such as allowances, the privileges of different ranks, and wearing swords.

It was a time of experimentation. Beginning in mid-1868, the work of building ministries and a bureaucracy to govern postshogunate Japan was under way. The councillor groups established departments responsible for military, financial, judicial, and foreign affairs. These developed over the coming decades into true national ministries on the European model. A special bureaucracy was set up to handle the affairs of Shinto— identified by pre-restoration visionaries and scholars as Japan's native religion and an essential part of its national rebirth. Buddhism, which had been an instrument of state control for the Tokugawa, was out of favor.

Shinto was purged of Buddhist influences. The government's close relationship with Shinto would be an important part of a developing nationalism among the Japanese. What came to be termed State Shinto was both supported and used by the government to foster patriotism based on reverence for the emperor.

The daimyo would not long keep their domains, even those who had supported the restoration. The young leaders who increasingly dominated government councils were coming to the conclusion that Japan, even with the supreme authority of the emperor restored, could never become a modern and unified nation on a feudal foundation.

The first step was to establish a truly national government. A crucial example was set in early 1869. In that year, the emperor accepted the "return" of Choshu, Satsuma, Hizen, and Tosa domains from their daimyo—to be followed within the year by others. Daimyo were allowed to keep part of their former incomes. Most were made governors of

"We now reverently offer up . . . our possessions and men. Let the Imperial commands be issued for . . . remodeling the territories of the various clans. Let the civil and criminal codes, the military laws . . . all proceed from the Emperor; let all the affairs of the Empire, great and small, be referred to him. After this, when the internal relations shall be upon a true footing, the Empire will be able to take its place side by side with the other countries of the world."

—*Memorial of the Daimyo of Choshu, Satsuma, Hizen, and Tosa, 1869* their former domains. Tosa, Satsuma, and Choshu domains allowed their military forces to form the basis of a new national army. This move helped the new government overcome serious challenges to its authority.

In 1871 a more confident national government replaced the daimyo with appointed governors and ordered the former daimyo to live in Tokyo on generous government pensions. The former domains were converted to prefectures. These later merged into forty-seven rural or urban administrative areas. Names of the restoration movement's battlegrounds and ideological hotbeds, such as Choshu and Satsuma, survived only on historical maps.

## SUNSET OF THE SAMURAI

Even though many samurai had supported the restoration, they faced a much harder fate than the daimyo. The lower- and middle-class samurai from the southwestern domains who controlled the early Meiji government knew about social barriers to talent and ability and wanted to reduce class distinctions. They moved to eliminate the old classes, defined by occupation, and consolidate samurai ranks. Commoners heard to their astonishment that they need no longer grovel before samurai. The new government suggested to the still armed, dangerous, and numerous samurai that they stop wearing swords and engage in useful professions. There were warnings that even the samurai's clothes and his unique topknot would have to give way to Western styles.

With the end of the domains, the samurai no longer had lords to serve or positions in which to serve them. Samurai incomes were replaced by inadequate government pensions. Later these became one-time payments. Most devastating to samurai as a class was the Conscription Act of January 1873. All males of military age—commoners included—could be called for military service for three years, on the model of continental Europe's conscript armies. Japan's old warrior class had lost its very reason for being.

The new government's military planners, such as Yamagata Aritomo, wanted to create a large military with modern discipline, tactics, and equipment to match the forces of the West. Equally important, they wanted an army answering only to the national government, not to lords or domains. It had to be an army that could deal firmly with challenges to the government's authority.

Those challenges would not be long in coming. Many samurai bitterly resented the new government. They had a very different vision of the society they had hoped would emerge from the struggles of the restoration. They could not imagine that the result would be the destruction of their class and humiliating laws such as the 1876 ban on wearing swords in public. Under the new government, they were classed as former samurai, or *shizoku*.

Samurai discontent nearly went from being a domestic to an international problem. When Korea rejected Japanese demands to open itself through an agreement heavily favoring Japan, conservative samurai in the Meiji government such as Saigo Takamori demanded an invasion of Korea to avenge the insult and—echoing the 1590s—to give restless samurai a worthwhile and honorable outlet for their energies.

# THE REAL LAST SAMURAI

I am a boat
Given to my country.
If the winds blow, let them!
If the waves rise, let them!

—*Saigo Takamori, 1873*

For Saigo Takamori of Satsuma—restoration leader and military hero—the old samurai values of service, self-denial, and scholarship were joined with a fierce new patriotism. Like many other samurai leaders of the restoration, he had risen from obscurity and risked exile, prison, and death to restore the emperor and safeguard Japan's place in the world. Saigo's political skills and generalship had been essential in forging the Satsuma-Choshu alliance and leading pro-emperor cause to victory. However, peacetime politics proved frustrating. Saigo resigned from the Meiji government in 1873, when his dreams of foreign conquest were blocked by more cautious statesmen.

Back in Satsuma, Saigo opened schools teaching military science and traditional subjects to samurai. Satsuma samurai were furious at the abolition (cancellation) of their class privileges and their impoverishment by the Meiji government's financial reforms. The government worried about angry samurai seizing the Satsuma arsenal and sent forces to remove the weapons.

This provoked an uprising in early 1877 that Saigo reluctantly agreed to lead. Satsuma forces were well armed and aggressive. But their goals were unclear beyond restoring the samurai as a class. Saigo's army besieged a major castle on Kyushu, but a large government force pushed the rebels back into Kagoshima. Here, Saigo took his last stand—and committed seppuku—at the Battle of Shiroyama.

The Satsuma uprising was the basis for the 2003 film *The Last Samurai*. The movie offers mix of accurate and inaccurate history. The real rebel forces preferred to fight with modern weapons when they could, not swords and bows. It is doubtful that the Saigo Takamori character (Katsumoto) would need or want a foreigner to advise him on tactics or help him commit seppuku—not even Tom Cruise.

*This statue of Saigo Takamori stands in Ueno Park in Tokyo.*

Cooler heads warned against a war for which Japan was financially unprepared. The idea was voted down in the Council of State. Furious, Saigo Takamori and other conservative samurai resigned from the government. Several of them led uprisings among embittered southwestern samurai, including the Saga Rebellion of 1874 and the Satsuma Rebellion of 1877 (led by Saigo). All were overwhelmed by government forces.

## A CHANGING ECONOMY

The farmers who had formed the largest and most heavily controlled part of Japan's population did not immediately benefit from the collapse of the feudal order. Times were anything but good. Bad harvests in the first years of the restoration were one problem. Heavy taxes, always a complaint in rural areas, were another. With the new government desperately needing tax revenue and with few ways to raise it, farmers were not about to get a break. The old domain taxes collected in rice were replaced by national government taxes payable in cash, often at rates farmers felt were unfair. The lifting of feudal restrictions on buying and transferring land favored wealthier landowners but left poorer farmers without traditional protections against losing their land in bad times. Military conscription hit the poorest farmers hard, as they could not pay a fee to get their sons out of military service. Hundreds of rural protests broke out. The government eased some tax requirements, but rural poverty would continue as both a social and a political issue.

In the cities, the government kept taxes on business low to promote industrial development. As Japan stabilized politically, traditional industries—such as silk production—were mechanized and became important sources of foreign exchange. Workers, many of them women, were drawn from rural areas. Textile production greatly expanded, and textile exports increased. Heavy industries—such as shipbuilding—

In 1872 the Japanese government opened the first modernized factory, Tomioka Silk Mill. The women shown in this late-1800s print are making silk thread.

developed with the growth of Japanese commercial shipping and government encouragement. Japan's large cities began to develop into some of the world's most important industrial areas.

## FOREIGN QUESTIONS

Foreign relations were an urgent concern. The new leadership could be grateful to Great Britain for keeping the foreign powers neutral in the civil war to restore the emperor and for its willingness to deal with the restoration government. The new government improved relations with Europe and the United States by pledging to uphold treaties made with the shogunate and punishing outrages against foreigners. The leaders still hoped to end the most damaging and humiliating provisions of the unequal treaties, such as unfavorable tariffs and extraterritoriality, but this goal was not achieved for many decades.

To signal the new government's legitimacy and goodwill to the world, the great lords arranged an audience with the emperor for foreign representatives in 1868. This previously unimaginable gesture marked the end of the imperial policy of expulsion of foreigners as a policy goal. It became possible to revere the emperor without calling for expelling the barbarians.

The new government was cautious about involving foreign companies too directly in Japan's economy, preferring to promote Japanese-controlled businesses. Foreign shipping lines had done well in Japan in the 1860s, but they were eased out through government support of Japanese

"As we entered the room the Son of Heaven [Emperor Meiji] rose and acknowledged our bows. He was . . . a tall youth with a bright eye and clear complexion: his demeanor was very dignified, well becoming the heir of a dynasty many centuries older than any other sovereignty on the face of the globe. He was dressed in a white coat with long padded trousers of crimson silk trailing like a lady's court-train. His head-dress was . . . surmounted by a long, stiff flat plume of black gauze. . . . His eyebrows were shaved off and painted in high up on the forehead; his cheeks were rouged and his lips painted with red and gold. His teeth were blackened. It was no small feat to look dignified under such a travesty of nature."

—*A. B. Mitford, describing an audience with Emperor Meiji, 1868*

companies such as Mitsubishi. The Japanese government needed British financing, engineering, and materials to build Japan's first railroads. (Rails weren't produced domestically for decades.) Still, the goal was always for Japanese to develop in their country all the elements of a modern industrial economy. Japan avoided heavy reliance on foreign capital. Its leaders knew that debts gave imperialist powers an excuse to intervene. Japanese banks would finance much of Japan's economic growth and become some of the world's largest financial institutions.

# EDUCATION AND EXPERTISE

Education was a key to prosperity and national strength. The Charter Oath of 1868 stated as goals the pursuit of knowledge "all over the world" and allowing people to "achieve their aspirations," even if they were not from the privileged class of samurai and nobles. These goals were realized through a series of educational reforms beginning with the Educational Order of 1872. It called for a national system of compulsory (required) elementary education, including education for girls. The focus would no longer be teaching classics for an elite, but on teaching everyone the literacy, mathematics, and science needed to build a modern nation.

Students chosen by merit could continue on to secondary education. A select few were admitted to the prestigious new national universities. Private high schools and universities—some established by Christian missionaries (mainly from the United States)—increased educational opportunities, particularly for women.

In pursuing restoration goals expressed in the slogan "rich country, strong army," the new leadership could draw on the advice of a growing body of Japanese with Western experience. By the early 1870s, hundreds of Japanese had been to Europe or the United States for studies or on diplomatic and fact-finding missions. They provided crucial skills and international perspective for the new government. The Iwakura Mission, headed by former court noble Iwakura Tomomi, spent nearly two years studying technology, government, politics, and education in the United States and Europe. So many important government ministers and officials went on the Iwakura Mission that a caretaker government had to be appointed to manage in their absence.

An important figure among educators and modernizers with Western experience was Fukuzawa Yukichi. Even before the restoration, his observations on Western life and institutions reached a wide audience. Fukuzawa went on to found Keio University, Japan's first private university. Fukuzawa was a major influence in explaining Western culture as Japanese attitudes toward the West changed from fear to admiration and curiosity.

Iwakura Tomomi, one of Emperor Meiji's advisers, led the Iwakura Mission.

Another pioneering educator was Tsuda Umeko. As a child, she went on the 1871 Iwakura Mission and remained in the United States for her education. Tsuda later founded a women's school that later became Tsuda University in Tokyo.

Foreign experts were hired in key fields such as industry and education with the goals of quickly setting up factories and schools and training Japanese to run them. Their impact was considerable, particularly in education.

This massive borrowing of Western technology, institutions, and expertise has been compared to Japan's earlier import of Chinese culture. Both helped shape Japan, but they did not replace Japanese culture or make Japan's people any less Japanese. Noting Western influences on Japanese culture in areas such as dress, architecture, and even food and the arts, foreign observers commented on how much and how well the Japanese were learning from the West. Sometimes they were accused of imperfectly imitating Western ways. This gave rise to a stereotype of the Japanese as copiers but not creators.

## THE MEIJI CONSTITUTION

After studying Western societies and governments, Meiji leaders decided it was important for Japan to have a formal constitution—a statement of the rights and obligations of Japan's people and government, as well as a plan for the government's basic structure and functions. They realized that Japan's constitution would also have to address the role of the emperor. The document that emerged embodied many hopes of the restoration. Imperial loyalists and nationalists could take pleasure in the central role provided for the emperor, while modernizers could take satisfaction that the constitution defined the rights of citizens and organized an efficient, centralized government structure.

The constitution was presented in 1889 as a gift to the people from the emperor, whose semi-divine essence and imperial lineage are described in the preamble. The first seventeen articles spell out the rights of the emperor—such as heading the armed forces. The constitution makes clear that all government power stems from these rights. The

In this woodcut, Emperor Meiji (center, standing) presides over the ceremony of the proclamation of the Meiji Constitution in 1889.

rights of subjects come second, in fifteen articles. Other chapters and articles establish a framework for a judiciary and a representative government, with an elected lower house and an upper house of appointed peers (nobles and other men of distinction).

Although it provided for a national assembly, Japan's first constitution was not created through a democratic process. It represented the careful work of senior statesmen such as Ito Hirobumi. While in Europe studying Western governments, Ito came to admire Germany. Germany's "Iron Chancellor," Otto von Bismarck, had recently used Prussian military power to unite the divided German states into an empire. The German system had a strong role for an emperor, a

"The advent [arrival] of Commodore Perry, followed by a rapid succession of great events . . . roughly awakened us to the consciousness of mighty forces at work to change the face of the outside world. We were ill prepared to bear the brunt of these forces, but once awakened to the need, were not slow to grapple with them. So, first of all, the whole fabric of the feudal system, which with its obsolete shackles and formalities hindered us in every branch of free development, had to be uprooted and destroyed."

—Ito Hirobumi, 1908

modern legal code, and efficient government institutions. With the powers of its representative government carefully limited in its national assembly, or diet, the German Empire seemed a better model for Japan than the unruly liberal democracies of Great Britain and France. Ito hired German scholars and brought them to Japan to advise on Japan's constitution. The constitution that resulted reflects its framers' reservations about unlimited democracy.

Still, Japan had a constitution and the institutions of a modern government. Although decision-making in Japan would be less democratic and more a process shared within a top leadership than in the Western democracies, the Meiji Constitution was clearly an impressive achievement. A short fourteen years earlier, Saigo Takamori had died to preserve ancient class privileges in the last stand of feudalism.

Two other important documents were part of Meiji

nation building. These were rescripts (declarations, or highly formal messages) from the emperor himself. The Imperial Rescript to Soldiers and Sailors of 1882 established a direct—and sacred—bond between the emperor and Japan's men in uniform. The emperor was the soul of the nation and was owed absolute loyalty and obedience even to death. It promoted a feeling of national identity and patriotism that helped fuel Japan's rise as a military power.

Like the Rescript to Soldiers and Sailors, the Imperial Rescript on Education of 1890 used Confucian concepts of duty to convey the importance of education and the emperor's central role in the nation. Copies of the rescript were displayed prominently in classrooms and treated with ritual respect. Compulsory, nationwide education was developed to teach the knowledge and skills needed to build a modern economy. It was also used to teach children their duties to Japan's society and its emperor.

# CHAPTER NINE
# EMPIRE, DEFEAT, AND REBIRTH

May the reign of the Emperor

Continue for a thousand, nay, eight thousand generations

And for the eternity that it takes

For small pebbles to grow into a great rock

And become covered with moss.

—"Kimi ga Yo," Japanese national anthem

As Japan developed a modern economy and its government and educational institutions took shape, the Japanese could feel growing pride in their nation's achievements. The economy had moved from light industries such as textiles to the heavy industries that were the backbone of an industrialized nation's strength in that era, such as steel, coal, and shipbuilding. Railroads and other transportation improvements joined the nation's cities. At the dawn of the twentieth century, it seemed that the hopes of the restoration were being realized.

Living standards rose, particularly in the cities, and great corporations prospered. But Japan's leaders never forgot the prime reason for Japan's urgent industrialization, expressed in the slogan, "rich country, strong army." Material progress would ensure Japan's military strength, her independence, and her standing among the nations of the world. As the twentieth century approached, Japan had more than met the threat of a foreign takeover. Soon she would become the dominant power in eastern Asia.

In 1894 to 1895, Japan defeated China, long the major power in eastern Asia. Japan's modern forces smashed the poorly led and badly equipped Chinese. The war was fought mainly over the question of who would dominate Korea, but Japan also gained the island of Taiwan and the Pescadores Islands, along with a cash indemnity. The war was enormously popular in Japan.

An even more satisfying victory was achieved over the creaking Russian Empire in 1904 to 1905. Japanese forces successfully captured Russian-held Port Arthur in China and defeated the Russian fleet at the Tsushima Strait. Japan was rewarded with more privileges in northern China, such as railway rights, and possessions in the Russian islands north of Hokkaido. Once humiliated by the superior military might of foreigners, Japan had now come full circle and could humble the two largest empires in Asia.

Thanks to its new economic and military strength, Japan had earned a place among the world's powers. In the Boxer Rebellion (1900–1901), an antiforeign uprising in China,

Japanese troops helped rescue foreigners besieged in Beijing, fighting alongside the Western troops their grandfathers had once feared as long-nosed devils.

Korea had been under diplomatic and military pressure from Japan since soon after the restoration. By 1910 Japan had forcibly annexed Korea and ruled it as part of Greater Japan. After joining the successful Allies in World War I (1914–1918), Japan also gained control of a German naval base (Shantung) in China and German-ruled islands in the western Pacific.

Emperor Taisho was born in 1878. He was the fifth son of Emperor Meiji.

By the end of World War I, Japan had a growing industrial economy to equip its modern fleets and armies. The great corporations mainly benefited from the growth, but it also produced an expanding urban middle class. Democracy even seemed to blossom briefly as the number of men eligible to vote increased during the 1912 to 1926 reign of Emperor Taisho. Women were not allowed to vote until after World War II (1939–1945).

Not everyone enjoyed prosperity and progress. Rural poverty continued to be a severe problem. Urban workers suffered when important Japanese industries were hard-hit by economic downturns in the 1920s and 1930s.

In the 1930s, Japan came under the influence of leaders who felt that the country's survival depended on further expanding Japanese power and control in Asia. The resources of Siberia and Southeast Asia beckoned, but the real prize remained China.

The opportunity was there. China was weak. After a 1911 revolution that had overthrown the Manchu dynasty, China slid into political chaos. While the Western powers were distracted by the bloodbath of World War I in Europe, Japan in 1915 presented its "Twenty-one Demands" to China, to gain more political, economic, and military control of that country. Some demands were reduced through U.S. intervention, but China had to agree to humiliating concessions.

In the 1920s, the Chinese Nationalists—or Kuomintang—led by Chiang Kai-shek gradually overcame regional warlords to assume control over much of China. The Kuomintang and the Chinese Communist Party led by Mao Zedong had been both allies and rivals in the movement to unite China and free it from foreign domination. But in 1927, Chiang turned on the Chinese Communists. Thanks to these political rivalries, China's weakness, and Japanese military strength, Japan joined the Western powers exploiting China. Japanese citizens had already set up profitable businesses in China's foreign-controlled ports and on China's great rivers. Japan wanted more.

The first target of expanded Japanese influence in China

was Manchuria. It became a Japanese economic colony, providing resources Japan lacked. Japanese-controlled railroads in Manchuria needed Japanese troops to guard them. Strong forces of the Imperial Japanese Army were stationed in Manchuria to protect and advance Japanese interests. Known as the Kwantung Army (named for an area in Manchuria), these forces took over all Manchuria in 1931 under ultranationalist Japanese officers acting on their own. In response to foreign protests of its actions through the League of Nations—the international body formed after World War I to prevent further wars—Japan left the league.

## MILITARY MIGHT

Japanese *zaibatsu*, or industrial groups, moved into Manchuria and set up industries. Sending Japanese colonists to Manchuria could relieve the pressure of Japan's growing population on the country's limited farmland. Emigration overseas—particularly to the United States—was blocked in part because of new restrictions on Japanese immigrants.

In Japan, influence in government belonged to military men. The 1889 Meiji Constitution provided for cabinet ministers appointed by the emperor rather than selected by political parties in the Diet. The genro, or senior statesmen, had been young men at the time of the Meiji Restoration, and they had long dominated Japan's national leadership. These men were nationalists who wished to advance Japanese power and interests. Some wanted a special role for the military, but they had largely led the country as civilians.

By the 1930s, however, senior officers of Japan's army and

navy were being appointed to head the ministries controlling the armed services. These officers reported directly to the emperor, and they dominated the government. As nationalist sentiment rose and nationalist propaganda increased, the military seemed to have solutions to Japan's domestic and foreign problems. It became difficult for civilian politicians to oppose the military leaders.

The Meiji Restoration had freed the energies of Japan's merchant class and made businessmen of former samurai. New wealth became concentrated in zaibatsu industrial combines such as Mitsui and Mitsubishi, the backbone of Japan's growing heavy industries.

Some in the military wanted to expand Japan's empire to control the badly needed resources that would help Japan's economy grow. Japanese nationalism came to include a sense that Japan had a special destiny, particularly in Asia. Some leaders felt that Japan, as the first modern Asian power, had a duty to lead Asia in expelling the Western powers. Only then could the region be prosperous and free—under Japanese leadership.

This powerful mix of economic, social, and nationalist beliefs was fueled by the younger officers who were members of secret societies and associations. Assassinations and military coup attempts by young officers in the 1930s took place in an increasingly violent political climate. In 1937 Japan invaded China outright.

The major powers were distracted by the rise of Nazi leader Adolf Hitler and fascism in Europe. Just as Britain and the United States began to focus on Japanese ambitions in Asia and the Pacific, World War II began in 1939.

The war provided more opportunities for Japanese expansion. The Netherlands and France, defeated by Germany in 1940, had little hope of defending their colonial possessions in the Dutch East Indies (modern Indonesia) and French Indochina (modern Vietnam, Cambodia, and Laos). Great Britain, fighting Germany and Italy, could spare few resources to defend its Asian interests from its base at Singapore.

The vast Asian lands and resources of the Soviet Union (a union of fifteen republics that included Russia) also tempted the Japanese militarists. The Soviet Union was weakened because the suspicious Soviet dictator Joseph Stalin had purged (killed) hundreds of the Red Army's best officers. Despite a temporary pact with Germany and cooperating with the Nazis in overrunning and dividing up Poland, the Soviets had to rebuild their forces to face a likely German threat from the west.

Expansionist leaders in the Japanese military were divided between those—mainly in the army—who wanted to attack the Soviet Union and seize its Asian territories and others—mainly in the navy—who wanted to strike south to control the oil of the Dutch East Indies. Seeking allies against the Communist Soviet Union, Japan had joined Germany in an anti-Communist pact in 1936.

Japanese militarists saw the Western presence in Asia and the Pacific as an encirclement that would prevent Japanese expansion and block access to vital resources. The United States was considered the biggest threat to Japanese plans. To prevent a U.S. reaction to their aggression in Asia, Japan threatened the United States by joining Germany and Italy in the Axis Pact of 1940.

Representatives of the Japanese, German, and Italian governments meet to sign the Axis Pact in 1940.

# THE WAR IN THE PACIFIC

After crushing defeats by Soviet forces in 1938 and 1939 in clashes over the border between Japanese-controlled Manchuria (called Manchukuo) and Soviet-dominated Mongolia, Japan had abandoned hopes of taking over Soviet lands in Asia. The Soviet-Japan Neutrality Pact was concluded in April 1941. Japan was free to turn its attention to China and Southeast Asia.

As the China crisis worsened, the United States put pressure on Japan to end the fighting. Japanese leaders worried about threats of economic actions by the United States. Japanese forces went on to complete their military occupation of French Indochina in June 1941, putting it closer to its goal of controlling the oil of the Dutch East Indies. It then threatened British-controlled Malaya (modern Malaysia) and the U.S.-controlled Philippines. U.S. reaction was swift. The United States blocked shipments of oil and iron to Japan. Japanese assets in the United States were frozen (held up in U.S. banks). Japan's military leaders began to plan war against the United States and the European powers in Asia partly to prevent the encirclement of Japan, to control resources in southeast Asia—above all, oil—and to maintain a free hand in China.

As in previous wars, Japanese planners hoped to gain major concessions through negotiation after early, overwhelming victories. In December 1941, Japanese forces attacked U.S., British, and Dutch possessions in Asia and the Pacific. Rather than being intimidated by Japan's surprise attack on Pearl Harbor in the U.S. Hawaiian Islands, Americans reacted with outrage and cries for vengeance. The United States quickly declared war on Japan. In response, Germany and Italy declared war on the United States in support of Japan, their Axis ally.

The strong military created under the Meiji Restoration performed superbly. Battle-hardened Japanese forces made easy conquests in Southeast Asia and the southwest Pacific. Allied resistance stiffened, however, and Japan was soon on the defensive. In three bloody years, the United States fought its way back across the Pacific. By late 1944, Allied forces were steadily retaking Western possessions held by the Japanese and going on to threaten Japanese territory.

Chinese and Japanese armies ranged back and forth across China in fierce battles. From bases in the recently captured Marianas Islands in the Pacific, U.S. long-range B-29 bombers flew firebombing raids that ravaged Japan's major cities. A relentless U.S. submarine campaign sank much of Japan's shipping and crippled the Japanese economy. In August 1945, the shock of U.S. bombings of Hiroshima and Nagasaki with atom bombs and a Soviet declaration of war against Japan brought home the hopelessness of Japan's position.

Hirohito, grandson of Meiji, had become emperor in 1926. His reign, Showa, meaning "Enlightened Peace," had known little peace. Instead, his people had been led down the path to militarism and a long and bloody war. It looked like they would have to endure unimaginable suffering as the United States fulfilled U.S. president Harry Truman's promise of "prompt and utter destruction." The emperor broke a deadlock in the cabinet and told his ministers to accept the terms for ending the war that the Allies had presented earlier.

Diehard military leaders in the cabinet saw the declaration's demand for unconditional surrender as the end of Japan as a nation centered on the emperor. They felt it would be better for all Japanese to die fighting. However, last-minute exchanges with the Allies hinted that the Japanese could retain the emperor as sovereign and determine their own political future.

"The Emperor shall be the symbol of the State and of the unity of the people, deriving his position from the will of the people, with whom resides sovereign power."

—*Showa Constitution, 1946*

Minister Namoro Shigomitso signs agreements on behalf of Emperor Hirohito at a formal ceremony of surrender in 1945. The ceremony took place on board the U.S.S. Missouri in Tokyo Bay.

At noon on August 15, 1945, the emperor's subjects heard his voice for the first time as he told them in a recorded radio message to "endure the unendurable" and "bear the unbearable." From the emperor's indirect and highly formal message, the Japanese learned that they had lost the war—a war, he claimed, Japan had been forced to fight for national survival and to liberate Asia from Western domination. The emperor expressed regret for the suffering of his people, particularly from the enemy's "cruel bombs." He implied that the war must end to spare Japan and the entire world further atomic devastation.

Some of the emperor's listeners knelt weeping near

the very gate where, only eight decades earlier, his newly restored grandfather Meiji had been carried past his awed subjects into the former shogun's palace. The Meiji Restoration had transformed Japan economically and socially. The Japanese reaction against foreigners forcibly opening their country had helped turn Japan into both an economic powerhouse and a regional troublemaker.

Western armies occupied a devastated Japan. On September 2, 1945, the official surrender document was signed on a U.S. battleship, the U.S.S. *Missouri*, amidst a vast allied fleet, in the same Tokyo Bay entered so boldly by Perry's wooden steamships ninety-two years earlier. Perry's flag was displayed above the signing ceremony as a pointed reminder.

## JAPANS'S FUTURE

Japan's rapid modernization and military strength had enabled her to turn on her neighbors. Because power was concentrated in the hands of a small number of powerful leaders, the political institutions developed after the Meiji Restoration were too weak to stop the reckless militarists who dominated Japan's government in the 1930s. The genuine patriotism that contributed to building a modern society and state in Japan also made Japan's moves to control other parts of Asia popular. The result was a tragedy for Japan and the world it helped bring to war.

Heavy-handed Japanese rule in Korea and the ravages of Japanese armies in China left a legacy of bitterness that affects politics and popular feeling in the twenty-first century. Asian governments periodically demand apologies for Japanese atrocities including the forced prostitution of Korean "comfort women" during World War II. Some Japanese leaders still try to deny or downplay these issues. Meanwhile, major Japanese politicians continue to pay visits to Yasukuni, a Shinto shrine in Tokyo established by Emperor Meiji for the souls of those who had died fighting for the emperor since 1868. Because the names of more than two million dead from World War II listed at the shrine include a small number of war criminals, the visits of Japanese public officials to Yasukuni Shrine cause anger in Asian countries that suffered under the Japanese.

The Japan that rose from defeat and devastation after World War II was in many ways a different country. Hirohito was forced to renounce his identity as a living god. But he remained as an important symbol of unity during the years that Allied troops occupied Japan and during the political and economic changes that followed. Ruling Japan much like a modern shogun, U.S. general Douglas MacArthur, Supreme Commander of the Allied Powers, appreciated the symbolic value of the emperor and shielded him from demands that he be tried as a war criminal.

"He was an Emperor by inherent birth, but in that instant I knew I faced the First Gentleman of Japan in his own right."

—General Douglas MacArthur,
on first meeting with Emperor Hirohito, 1945

The new Japanese constitution renounced war, and Japan became a more democratic country and the closest ally of the United States in Asia. Above all, Japanese poured their energies and talents into rebuilding their country and economy. Emperor Akihito, Hirohito's son, reigns over a land that is peaceful and wealthy beyond the imaginations of the men and women who dedicated and gave their lives to his great-grandfather, the Emperor Meiji.

*Emperor Akihito and Empress Michiko appear at a ceremony in Japan in 2008.*

# PRIMARY SOURCE RESEARCH

To learn about historical events, people study many sources, such as books, websites, newspaper articles, photographs, and paintings. These sources can be separated into two general categories—primary sources and secondary sources.

A primary source is the record of an eyewitness. Primary sources provide firsthand accounts about a person or event. Examples include diaries, letters, autobiographies, speeches, newspapers, and oral history interviews. Libraries, archives, historical societies, and museums often have primary sources available on-site or on the Internet.

A secondary source is published information that was researched, collected, and written or otherwise created by someone who was not an eyewitness. These authors or artists use primary sources and other secondary sources in their research, but they interpret and arrange the source material in their own works. Secondary sources include history books, novels, biographies, movies, documentaries, and magazines. Libraries and museums are filled with secondary sources.

After finding primary and secondary sources, authors and historians must evaluate them. They may ask questions such as: Who created this document? What is this person's point of view? What biases might this person have? How trustworthy is this document? Just because a person was an eyewitness to an event does not mean that person recorded the whole truth about that event. For example, a soldier describing a battle might depict only the heroic actions of his unit and only the brutal behavior of the enemy. An account from a soldier on the opposing side might portray the same battle very differently. When sources disagree, researchers must decide through additional study which explanation makes the most sense. For this reason, historians consult a variety of primary and secondary sources. Then they can draw their own conclusions.

The Pivotal Moments in History series takes readers on a journey to important junctures in history that shaped our modern world. Authors research each event using both primary and secondary sources, an approach that enhances readers' awareness of the complexities of the materials and helps bring to life the rich stories from which we draw our understanding of our shared history.

## PRIMARY SOURCE IMAGES

We have many sources of visual images to help us understand the events involved in the Meiji Restoration. The drawings and paintings of Westerners arriving in Japan provide an American or European perspective. Western governments of the time often sent official artists on important diplomatic, military, or exploring expeditions to provide detailed drawings and paintings. Perry's expedition came at a time when photography was developing quickly, but problems with heavy equipment and long poses of the time made photography impractical in many situations. Photos of people and events became more common in the 1860s and later. Some were hand-colored (tinted) to change the black and white to color.

A samurai poses in a studio with his weapons and daily garb. Note the two swords. The photo, dating to the late 1800s, has been hand-tinted and other versions may be colored differently.

Japanese photographer Uchida Kuichi took the official imperial portrait of the young Emperor Meiji in 1873. As always, the emperor appears in military uniform.

This image of an important official at the site of Perry's landing portrays the samurai in a somber setting, dignified and serious—and all business with their swords at hand. The original photograph was taken by a member of Perry's crew in about 1853. An American artist used that picture to create this lithograph (print) for a book.

Finally, we have the Japanese view of things expressed through Japanese prints. The art of making ukiyo-e—woodblock prints—reached its height during the late Edo period in Japan. Pressing an ink-covered wooden plate, or block for

*Perry's officers are portrayed by the Japanese as a bit frightening—grimacing and hairy. This picture of a naval commander comes from a series showing types of Americans. These "news of the day" descriptions were widely copied and distributed to a curious Japanese public. Some depictions of the Americans and their ships were downright terrifying.*

each color onto a picture outline, artists such as Utagawa Hiroshige (also known as Ando Hiroshige) and Katsushika Hokusai created masterpieces of composition and color on themes such as famous landscapes and the passing seasons.

This wood-block print shows farmers planting rice. Behind them, travelers walk along the Tokaido Highway. Master printmaker Ando Hiroshige created this image in 1855 for a series called "The Fifty-Three Stations of the Tokaido."

*This print from the late 1800s portrays Commodore Perry's flagship as a black ship with monstrous faces at its prow and stern. The creator of this image is not known.*

Other prints reflected daily life or important events of the day. As the Meiji period progressed, Japan's modernization, the exploits of Japan's military, and even the emperor became favorite subjects.

# TIMELINE

**710–794**    Emperors rule Japan from Nara.

**794–1185**    Imperial power shifts to Kyoto and then declines.

**1185–1333**    The Minamoto family establishes Japan's first line of shoguns. Imperial power is briefly restored in 1333.

**1336–1573**    As the shogunate weakens, Japan slides into chaos and lords of warring states fight for regional power.

**1543**    European contacts and trade begin as the Portuguese introduce guns and Christianity.

**1573–1598**    Oda Nobunaga and Toyotomi Hideyoshi bring daimyo under control, centralize government authority, and regulate society.

**1603**    Tokugawa Ieyasu becomes shogun after his victory at Sekigahara in 1600. Japan is unified under the Tokugawas.

**1635–1639**    The Tokugawas close Japan to foreigners. Limited trade is allowed with the Dutch and Chinese. Christianity is outlawed.

**1853–1854**    U.S. commodore Matthew Perry's four warships arrive at Uraga. Perry delivers a U.S. request for a treaty. When Perry returns after several months with more ships, shogunate officials sign the

Convention of Kanagawa. Discontent over the Perry treaty fuels the movement to "revere the emperor and expel the barbarians."

1858  The Treaty of Amity and Commerce opens some Japanese ports to trade and limits Japanese control of tariffs and foreign nationals, outraging many Japanese.

1859  Killings of foreigners begin.

1860  Ii Naosuke is assassinated for signing foreign treaties and suppressing the shogunate's opponents.

1861–1862  Attacks on shogunate leaders and foreigners continue. The shogunate tries to appease treaty opponents. British businessman Charles Richardson is killed by Satsuma samurai.

1863  Important daimyo pressure the shogunate to cooperate with the emperor. The emperor demands the expulsion of foreigners. The shogun journeys to Kyoto to show cooperation with the emperor. The shogunate tries to "unite court and shogun" through marriage. In June the Choshu domain attacks foreign ships. In August the British bombard the Satsuma domain to avenge Richardson's killing. In September in Kyoto, antiforeign extremists are suppressed and Choshu forces expelled.

**1864**　In August Choshu pro-emperor forces trying to seize the Imperial Palace are driven from Kyoto. The emperor orders the shogunate to punish Choshu. In September, Western powers defeat Choshu and open the straits of Shimonoseki. Choshu conservatives suppress radicals, and the shogunate expedition against Choshu is ended.

**1865**　Rebels seize Choshu. In November, under pressure from the shogunate and European powers, the emperor approves port openings.

**1866**　In March Choshu and Satsuma form a secret alliance. In the Summer War, a shogunate expedition to punish Choshu is repelled. In August, Shogun Iemochi dies. Late in the year, Emperor Komei dies.

**1867**　In January Tokugawa Yoshinobu is made shogun. In February Mutsuhito becomes emperor. In July to October, a southwestern coalition against the shogunate forms. In November Yoshinobu gives up shogunal powers but still controls Tokugawa forces and lands.

**1868**　In January pro-emperor forces seize the Imperial Palace. The restoration of imperial rule is announced. Yoshinobu's forces advance toward Kyoto to protest moves against the Tokugawas. He is defeated and flees to Edo. In March through

| | |
|---|---|
| | April, southwestern domain forces under the imperial banner move north and take Edo. The Charter Oath of 1868 is proclaimed. In October the Meiji reign begins. In November the last Tokugawa forces in northern Honshu surrender. |
| 1869 | In April Edo becomes the new imperial capital. In June resistance ends in Hokkaido. In July the daimyo return their domains to the emperor and are compensated. |
| 1871 | Modern prefectures replace domains. Samurai are abolished as a class. The Iwakura Mission studies governments and economies of the United States and Europe. |
| 1873 | Military conscription is introduced. |
| 1877 | A samurai rebellion in Satsuma is crushed by the Meiji government. |
| 1882 | The Imperial Rescript to Soldiers and Sailors is proclaimed. |
| 1889 | The emperor gives the Meiji Constitution to the people. |
| 1890 | The Imperial Rescript on Education is proclaimed. |
| 1894–1895 | Japan defeats China and seizes Taiwan. |
| 1900–1901 | Japanese forces help crush the Boxer Rebellion in China. |

**1904–1905** Japan wins the Russo-Japanese War.

**1910** Japan forcibly annexes Korea.

**1912** Emperor Meiji dies, and Emperor Taisho assumes the throne.

**1926** Meiji's grandson Hirohito becomes emperor and takes the name Showa for his reign.

**1931–1932** Japan takes over Manchuria.

**1937** Japan invades China.

**1941** Japan occupies French Indochina. Japan joins Axis powers Italy and Germany in fighting the Allies. Japan attacks Pearl Harbor and overruns U.S., British, and Dutch possessions in Asia.

**1945** The Allies retake many territories and prepare to invade Japan. Japan surrenders after the United States drops two atomic bombs and the Soviet Union enters the war. Japan is occupied by U.S. and Allied forces.

**1945–1952** Douglas MacArthur, the Supreme Commander of Allied Forces, reshapes many Japanese institutions. The emperor renounces his divinity in 1946. Japan creates a more democratic government with the emperor as its symbolic head. A new constitution renounces the right to make war and gives women the vote.

# GLOSSARY

**BUDDHISM:** a religion of Indian origin that was introduced to Japan through China and Korea about A.D. 550. Buddhism teaches transcendence over suffering and the material world. Buddhism became and is widely practiced in Japan in a number of sects such as Jodo, Zen, and Nichiren.

**CONFUCIANISM:** considered a religion by some, this ancient Chinese philosophy emphasizing virtue and hierarchy in social relationships strongly influenced Japanese attitudes toward the family, education, power, and leadership.

**COURT:** the officials, nobles, and retainers who surround and served a ruler. Tokugawa Japan had a shogunal court in Edo and an imperial court around the emperor in Kyoto.

**DAIMYO:** hereditary lords who ruled domains or territories

**EMPEROR:** the traditional and hereditary head of the Japanese nation. The emperor's role became largely spiritual and ceremonial after political power was taken by the shoguns. In Japanese the emperor is referred to as *tenno*, or "heavenly ruler."

**FEUDALISM:** a hereditary system of mutual obligation that evolved mainly to provide military service. A lord provided or guaranteed incomes or productive land to his samurai retainers, who in turn had to fight for him when called upon. All lords owed service to the shogun, who guaranteed their families their lands and defended them and the nation against enemies.

**SAMURAI:** the hereditary class of warriors who served their daimyo, or local chiefs. Samurai became the only class allowed to bear arms, and they traditionally carried two swords.

**SHINTO:** Shinto is based on the worship of spirits and places in nature. Some scholars in the decades before the restoration wanted the Japanese to return to Shinto as Japan's native religion. Shinto was promoted by the Meiji government and identified with the emperor.

**SHOGUN:** short for *seiidaishogun*, or "barbarian-conquering great general," shoguns were hereditary military rulers who controlled Japan politically and militarily from 1192 to 1867.

**SONNO JOI:** the radical samurai rallying cry to "revere the emperor and expel the barbarians" inspired political assassinations and terrorist killings of foreigners. Many sonno joi activists gave their lives fighting the shogunate.

**UNEQUAL TREATIES:** treaties favoring Western nations that were forced on militarily weaker countries. Terms often included extraterritoriality, or freedom for Westerners from being tried in local courts.

**VASSAL:** a member of the lower nobility who owed military service to a noble of higher rank. In turn, the great lord protected his vassals.

# WHO'S WHO?

**ABE MASAHIRO (1819–1857)** Head of the shogunate's senior councillors, Abe felt forced to give in to Perry's demands in 1854. Abe's weak handling of the crisis and his seeking of daimyo support for his decisions inflamed opposition to the shogunate.

**TOWNSEND HARRIS (1804–1878)** The United States's first consul in Japan, Harris pressured the shogunate into signing the Treaty of Amity and Commerce in 1858 and provoked an angry reaction from Japanese, who felt the Harris Treaty surrendered Japan's independence.

**HOTTA MASAYOSHI (1810–1864)** As the senior councillor of the shogunate, Hotta's response to Townsend Harris's demands for a trade agreement led to the Treaty of Amity and Commerce of 1858.

**II NAOSUKE (1815–1860)** Like Abe and Hotta, Ii Naosuke's main challenge leading the shogunate as *tairo* (great elder) was to satisfy the foreign powers' demands for treaties while handling angry antiforeign reaction. Ii made enemies by preventing Tokugawa Yoshinobu from becoming shogun while punishing Yoshinobu's supporters, treaty opponents, and pro-emperor activists. Ii was assassinated by Mito samurai.

**ITO HIROBUMI (1841–1909)** One of the young Choshu samurai who smuggled themselves out of Japan to study in Britain, Ito returned in 1864 and tried to warn Choshu that fighting the West was hopeless. Ito was active in bringing down the shogunate and took a key role in establishing the framework of the Meiji government. He studied Western economies and governments during the 1871 Iwakura Mission and on later tours of Europe. Ito's long service included preparing the 1889 Meiji Constitution and serving as prime minister. When Japan's 1905 victory over Russia allowed Japan to exert control over Korean affairs, Ito was made the top Japanese official in Korea. He was assassinated by a Korean nationalist in 1909.

**IWAKURA TOMOMI (1825–1883)** Tomomi was one of the few imperial court nobles who helped lead the restoration. He at first stirred up opposition to the treaties with the West in Kyoto but acted as a moderate working to unite the imperial court and the shogunate. Tomomi's enemies had him banned from Kyoto for being too proshogunate. However, Tomomi soon came to support the restoration movement and helped plan the January 1868 takeover of the Imperial Palace by pro-emperor domain forces. Tomomi held several important positions in the Meiji government and led the Iwakura Mission to study Western countries in 1871.

**KIDO KOIN (1833–1877)** This Choshu samurai became a pro-emperor radical after studying under Yoshida Shoin. He helped both to create the Satsuma-Choshu alliance and to establish the new Meiji government.

**KOMEI (1831–1867)** The last emperor to live in Kyoto, Komei was born Osahito. His reign began in 1846 after the death of his father, Emperor Ninko. Komei's strong opposition to admitting foreigners to Japan increasingly forced the shogunate to consult with him on treaty matters. Komei ordered the expulsion of foreigners in 1863 but eventually was convinced by the shogunate to accept the treaties. Komei was the symbol and the rallying point of the sonno joi movement to revere the emperor and expel the barbarians.

**MATSUDAIRA KATAMORI (1836–1893)** A Tokugawa relative and lord of Aizu domain, Matsudaira Katamori handled security matters in Kyoto for the shogunate from 1862 through its collapse and helped control pro-emperor radicals. His forces were among the last to hold out in northern Japan, finally surrendering after the siege of Aizu castle.

**MEIJI (1852–1912)** Born to a consort of Emperor Komei, Mutsuhito's adoption by the emperor's main consort put him in line for the throne. He grew up in the Imperial Palace in Kyoto and received a traditional education. Insulated from the events shaking Japan, Mutsuhito was barely a teenager when he succeeded to the throne on February 3, 1867. Political leadership for much of his reign was in the hands of an oligarchy (small ruling group) of restoration leaders, but the emperor took his duties seriously. He kept up an exhausting schedule of reviewing state papers as well as attending court functions, diplomatic events, and military inspections. Like many at the imperial court, he was an accomplished poet. He fathered fifteen children by ladies in waiting. (Meiji's chief consort was childless.) Among the five that survived childhood was Meiji's successor, Emperor Taisho, grandfather of Japan's current emperor.

**OKUBO TOSHIMICHI (1830–1878)** Along with fellow Satsuma leader Saigo Takamori, Toshimichi helped forge the Satsuma-Choshu alliance that brought down the shogunate. An important organizer of the new Meiji government, Toshimichi blocked Saigo's proposed invasion of Korea in 1873 and was instrumental in crushing the 1877 Satsuma Rebellion led by Saigo. Satsuma samurai assassinated Toshimichi in 1878.

**MATTHEW CALBRAITH PERRY (1794–1858)** With a long and distinguished naval career behind him, Perry commanded a U.S. expedition sent in 1853 to convince the Japanese to open relations with the United States. Mixing threats and diplomacy, Perry persuaded shogunate officials to agree to a U.S. treaty in 1854. Similar treaties with other countries followed, making many Japanese feel they were losing control of their country. The reaction to the forced opening of Japan, begun by Perry, led to the overthrow of the shogunate and the restoration of the emperor.

**SAIGO TAKAMORI (1827–1877)** A samurai serving the Satsuma government, Saigo was exiled for his radical views. He was later called on to command Satsuma domain forces suppressing Choshu radicals in Kyoto. Soon, however, Saigo turned against the shogunate and helped form the Satsuma-Choshu alliance. He led alliance forces in the campaigns of 1868 that ended Tokugawa power. Saigo did not completely support modernization. At heart a traditional samurai, Saigo had impractical ideas about how Japan could be governed and strengthened economically. He broke with the Meiji government in 1873. In Satsuma, Saigo became involved with resentful samurai and led the doomed 1877 Satsuma Rebellion.

**SAKAMOTO RYOMA (1835–1867)** A visionary who foresaw Japan shedding its feudal past and uniting under the emperor, Ryoma's radical activities and independent ways got him outlawed from his native Tosa domain. A shogunate official whom Ryoma nearly assassinated convinced Ryoma instead to help him develop a modern navy for Japan. In 1866 Ryoma arranged the formation of the Satsuma-Choshu alliance that would bring down the shogunate. He was killed by proshogun agents in 1867.

**SHIMAZU HISAMITSU (1817–1887)** Hisamitsu controlled Satsuma after 1858 as regent for his young son. He first hoped to bring the shogunate and imperial court closer but increasingly favored the pro-emperor cause. His support of the Satsuma-Choshu alliance and willingness to give up domain authority were crucial.

**TOKUGAWA IEMOCHI (1846–1866)** Upon his father Iesada's death in 1858, Tokugawa Iemochi inherited both the office of shogun and the crisis brought on by the foreign treaties. He had to marry Princess Kazinomiya in order to forge a political alliance with her brother, Emperor Komei. During Iemochi's short rule (1858–1866), the shogunate's political affairs were handled by senior officials.

**TOKUGAWA IESADA (1824–1858)** Shogun Tokugawa Iesada was thought to be mentally unfit to rule. During Iesada's time (1853–1858), senior councillors arranged treaties opening Japan to foreigners and provoked an angry reaction among nationalistic Japanese.

**TOKUGAWA IEYASU (1543–1616)** A brilliant general and a crafty political leader, Ieyasu expanded his power during the unification campaigns of Oda and Hideyoshi. After Hideyoshi's death, Ieyasu crushed rival lords at the Battle of Sekigahara in 1600. Made shogun in 1603, he passed his title to his son Hidetada in 1605 and oversaw Tokugawa affairs until his death in 1616. The Tokugawa dynasty founded by Ieyasu lasted until 1867.

**TOKUGAWA IEYOSHI (1793–1853)** Ieyoshi's rule (1837–1853) was marked by famines, uprisings, and increasing foreign incursions. Perry's forced opening of Japan deeply upset Ieyoshi and may have hastened his death.

**TOKUGAWA NARIAKI (1800–1860)** After retiring as daimyo of the Mito domain, Nariaki coordinated defenses for the shogunate and warned Japan to repel the foreign threat. He hoped to see the emperor restored to power. Nariaki tried to get his son Yoshinobu chosen to succeed shogun Iesada, but was blocked by Ii Naosuke.

**TOKUGAWA YOSHINOBU (1837–1913)** The son of pro-emperor, antiforeign Tokugawa Nariaki, Yoshinobu was proposed to succeed Iesada in 1858, but Ii Naosuke's faction made Iemochi shogun. Confined for a time as a threat to the shogunate, Yoshinobu was allowed to take on important roles in it and was made guardian to Iemochi. Yoshinobu worked to reform and strengthen the shogunate and improve relations with the imperial court and the daimyo. After Iemochi's death in 1866, Yoshinobu accepted the office of shogun. He resigned and returned his powers to the emperor in late1867 to prevent civil war. Protesting Satsuma-Choshu alliance moves to completely end the power of the Tokugawa house, Yoshinobu led his armies to defeat at Toba-Fushimi in late January 1868. Yoshinobu lived in retirement in Shizuoka into the twentieth century.

**YAMAGATA ARITOMO (1838–1922)** A samurai student of Yoshida Shoin, Yamagata fought for Choshu during the restoration movement. He helped create a new national army and helped introduce military conscription in 1873, strengthening the new government and ending the role of the samurai as Japan's fighting class. Yamagata was one of the last surviving genro, or elder statesman, who guided Japan for decades after the restoration. He favored aggressive policies toward Japan's neighbors and is often blamed for promoting militarism by making the army free from civilian control.

**YOSHIDA SHOIN (1830–1859)** A Choshu samurai, Shoin was a brilliant student. Both curious and concerned about the West, he failed in his attempt to go abroad on one of Perry's vessels and was punished by the shogunate.

Shoin's informal academy in Choshu shaped the views of other radicals—many of them future leaders in the Meiji government. Shoin was executed for plotting to assassinate a shogunate official.

# SOURCE NOTES

4 "Chinese Dynastic Record," quoted in David John Lu, ed. *Sources of Japanese History*, vol. 1 (New York: McGraw-Hill, 1974), 8.

16 "Edict of 1635 Ordering the Closing of Japan, Completion of the Exclusion, 1639," quoted in Lu, vol. 1, 216–218.

18 Isaac Titsingh, *Secret Memoirs of the Shoguns*, ed. Timon Screech (London: Routledge, 2006), 161.

23 Engelbert Kaempfer, *Kaempfer's Japan: Tokugawa Culture Observed*, trans. Beatrice M. Bodart-Bailey (Honolulu: University of Hawaii Press, 1998), 359.

27 Matsuo Basho, *The Narrow Road to the Deep North*, Date TK http://www.terebess.hu/english/haiku/basho2.html#32 (August 25, 2008).

30 Ryusaku Tsunoda, William Theodore de Bary, and Donald Keene, ed, *Sources of Japanese Tradition* (New York: Columbia University Press, 1958), 614.

37 Wilhelm Heine, *With Perry to Japan: A Memoir*, trans. Frederic Trautmann (Honolulu: University of Hawaii Press, 1990), 75.

46 Rutherford Alcock, *The Capital of the Tycoon, A Narrative of a Three Years' Residence in Japan*, vol. 1. May 9, 2007. http://books.google.com/books?hl=en&id=pHIzAAAAMAAJ&dq=The+Capital+of+the+Tycoon&printsec=frontcover&source=web&ots=MA1hMwPdkJ&sig=PTNVgriuTYtvLJUxepsmErjSpF4#PPR4,M1 (October 22, 2008).

47 Walt Whitman, "The Errand-Bearers," quoted in "US-Japan 150 Years," Consulate General of Japan in New York, (June 30, 2005) http://www.ny.us.emb-japan.go.jp/150th/html/kanrinE6.htm (October 22, 2008).

51 Fukuzawa Yukichi, *Autobiography of Yukichi Fukuzawa*, trans. Eiichi Kyooka (New York: Columbia University Press, 1980), 129.

53 Tokugawa Nariaki, "Observations on Coastal Defense," quoted in Lu, vol. 2, 9–10.

56 Alcock, 219–220.

58 Ernest Mason Satow, *A Diplomat in Japan* (Philadelphia: J. B. Lippincott

Company, 1921), 52.

62 Ibid., 87.

63 Arthur Lloyd, *Admiral Togo* (Tokyo: Kinkodo Publishing Co., 1905), 23–26.

64 Satow, 129.

68 Emperor Komei, quoted in Keene, 78.

82 "Letter of Saigo and Okubo on the Imperial Restoration, 1867," quoted in Lu, vol. 2, 29.

92 Algernon Bertram Mitford, *Mitford's Japan: Memories and Recollections 1866–1906*, ed. Hugh Cortazzi (London: Japan Library, 2002), 66–67.

94 Donald Keene, *Emperor of Japan: Meiji and His World, 1852–1912* (New York. Columbia University Press, 2002), 159.

96 "The Charter Oath of 1868," quoted in Tsunoda, de Bary, and Keene, 643.

99 "Memorial of the Daimyo of Choshu, Sastuma, Hizen, and Tosa," quoted in Mitford, 150.

102 Saigo Takamori, quoted in Liah Greenfeld, *The Spirit of Capitalism* (Cambridge: Harvard University Press, 2003), 285.

107 Mitford, 120.

112 Ito Hirobumi, "Reminiscences on the Drafting of the New Constitution," quoted in Tsunoda, de Bary, and Keene, 671.

114 *About.com Japanese Language*. Japanese National Anthem, n.d. http://japanese.about.com/library/weekly/aa030400.htm (October 20, 2008).

123 "The Showa Constitution, 1946," quoted in Lu, 2:194.

126 Douglas MacArthur, quoted in Robert Trumbull, "A Leader Who Took Japan to War, to Surrender, and Finally to Peace," *New York Times*, January 7, 1989. http://query.nytimes.com/gst/fullpage.html?res=950DE3D61F3CF934A35752C0A96F948260 (October 30, 2008).

# SELECTED BIBLIOGRAPHY

## PRIMARY SOURCES

Alcock, Rutherford. *The Capital of the Tycoon, a Narrative of a Three Years' Residence in Japan*. Vol. 1. (May 9, 2007) http://books.google.com/books?hl=en&id=pHIzAAAAMAAJ&dq=The+Capital+of+the+Tycoon&printsec=frontcover&source=web&ots=MA1hMwPdkJ&sig=PTNVg riuTYtvLJUxepsmErjSpF4#PPR4,M1 (October 22, 2008).

The Centre for East Asian Cultural Studies. *The Meiji Japan through Contemporary Sources*. Vol. 1. Tokyo: Centre for East Asian Cultural Studies, 1969.

Harris, Townsend. *The Complete Journal of Townsend Harris*. Introduction by Mario Emilio Cosenza. Rutland, VT: Charles E. Tuttle, 1959.

Hawks, Francis L., ed. *Commodore Perry and the Opening of Japan*. Stroud, UK: Nonsuch Publishing, 2005.

Heine, Wilhelm. *With Perry to Japan: A Memoir*. Translated by Frederic Trautmann. Honolulu: University of Hawaii Press, 1990.

Lu, David John, ed. *Sources of Japanese History*. Vol. 1–3. New York: McGraw Hill, 1974.

Mitford, Algernon Bertram. *Mitford's Japan: Memories and Recollections 1866–1906*. Edited by Hugh Cortazzi. London: Japan Library, 2002.

Satow, Ernest Mason. *A Diplomat in Japan*. Philadelphia: J. B. Lippincott, 1921.

Tsunoda, Ryusaku, William Theodore de Bary, and Donald Keene, ed. *Sources of Japanese Tradition*. New York: Columbia University Press, 1958.

## SECONDARY SOURCES

Akamatsu, Paul. *Meiji, 1868*. Translated by Miriam Kochan. New York: Harper and Row, 1972.

Beasley, W. G. *The Meiji Restoration*. Stanford, CA: Stanford University Press, 1972.

———. *The Rise of Modern Japan: Political, Economic and Social Change since 1850*. London: Weidenfeld & Nicolson, 2000.

Jansen, Marius B. *Sakamoto Ryoma and the Meiji Restoration*. Princeton, NJ: Princeton University Press, 1961.

———, ed. *The Emergence of Meiji Japan*. New York: Cambridge University Press, 1995.

Keene, Donald. *Emperor of Japan: Meiji and His World, 1852–1912*. New York: Columbia University Press, 2002.

Naval Historical Center. *Matthew C. Perry and the Opening of Japan*. March 23, 2004. http://www.history.navy.mil/library/special/perry_openjapan1.htm (October 22, 2008).

Ravina, Mark. *The Last Samurai: The Life and Battles of Saigo Takamori*. Hoboken, NJ: John Wiley & Sons, 2004.

Roberts, John G. *Black Ships and Rising Sun, the Opening of Japan to the West*. New York: Messner, 1971.

Totman, Conrad D. *The Collapse of the Tokugawa Bakufu, 1862–1868*. Honolulu: University Press of Hawaii, 1980.

———. *Japan before Perry: A Short History*. Berkeley: University of California Press, 1981.

Wathall, Anne. *The Weak Body of a Useless Woman: Matsuo Taseko and the Meiji Restoration*. Chicago: University of Chicago Press, 1998.

Wilson, George. *Patriots and Redeemers in Japan: Motives in the Meiji Restoration*. Chicago: University of Chicago Press, 1992.

# FURTHER READING AND WEBSITES

## BOOKS

Behnke, Alison. *Japan in Pictures*. Minneapolis: Twenty-First Century Books, 2003.

Buruma, Ian. *Inventing Japan, 1853–1964*. New York: Modern Library, 2003.

Hanley, Susan. *Everyday Things in Premodern Japan: The Hidden Legacy of Material Culture*. Berkeley: University of California Press, 1997.

Museum of Fine Arts, Boston. *Japan at the Dawn of the Modern Age: Woodblock Prints from the Meiji Era, 1868–1912*. Boston: Museum of Fine Arts, Boston, 2001.

Totman, Conrad. *A History of Japan*. Oxford: Blackwell Publishers, 2000.

Traganou, Jilly. *The To–kaido Road: Traveling and Representation in Edo and Meiji Japan*. New York: RoutledgeCurzon, 2004.

Williams, Barbara. *World War II: Pacific*. Minneapolis: Twenty-First Century Books, 2005.

## WEBSITES

*Japan: Memoirs of a Secret Empire*
http://www.pbs.org/empires/japan/theprogram.html
This PBS companion provides a good overview of cultural and political developments in the Edo period.

*Meiji Restoration*
http://www.virtualmuseum.ca/Exhibitions/Meiji/english/html/index.html
This interactive tour describes daily life, culture, and important events in Meiji times.

*Metadatabase of Old Japanese Photographs in Bakamatsu-Meiji Periods*
http://oldphoto.lb.nagasaki-u.ac.jp/en/
This site offers an extensive collection of period photos, many hand-tinted.

*National Diet Library*
http://www.ndl.go.jp/en/index.html
The English version of this official Japanese government site offers a

wealth of information in several sections. Modern Japan in Archives provides samples of original Japanese documents along with English explanations as well as a chronological table. Portraits of Modern Japanese Historical Figures show many of the leaders of the restoration and Meiji era. The Meiji and Taisho Eras in Photographs and Scenic Mementos of Japan offer a picture of daily life during these periods.

*Naval Historical Center*
http://www.history.navy.mil/search/
This U.S. Department of the Navy site provides information on the Perry Expedition, the Shimonoseki Incident, and other late Edo and Meiji Restoration events.

*Visualizing Cultures*
http://ocw.mit.edu/ans7870/21f/21f.027/home/index.html
This site explores Japanese and Western images of events from Perry's arrival through World War II and provides thoughtful commentary along with useful links.

## FICTION

Clavell, James. *Gai-Jin*. New York: Delacorte Press, 1993.

————. *Shogun: A Novel of Japan*. New York: Atheneum, 1977.

Wiley, Richard. *Commodore Perry's Minstrel Show*. Austin: University of Texas Press, 2007.

## FILMS

*The Last Samurai*. Directed by Edward Zwick. Warner Bros., 2003. Loosely based on Saigo Takamori's role in the Satsuma Rebellion, this Hollywood epic re-creates the clash of the Meiji government's rapid modernization with traditional samurai ways.

*Seven Samurai*. Directed by Akira Kurosawa. Toho Co., 1954. A classic of world cinema about the changing role of the samurai.

*The Twilight Samurai* or (*Tasogare Seibei*). Directed by Yoji Yamada. Hakuhodo, 2002. Set at the end of the Edo period, this film offers swordplay and a look at the life of a poor rural samurai.

# INDEX

159

# ABOUT THE AUTHORS

Mark E. Cunningham majored in history and political science at the University of Iowa and received an MA in English as a second language at the University of Northern Arizona. A former Peace Corps volunteer, he has lived and worked all over the world. Mark teaches at Michigan State University.

Lawrence J. Zwier is the associate director of the English Language Center at Michigan State University. He wrote *The Persian Gulf and Iraq Wars* for Lerner Publishing Group.

# PHOTO ACKNOWLEDGMENTS